TRAVELLERS

COSTA RICA

By
THEA MACAULAY

Written by Thea Macaulay

Original photography by Danny Levy Sheehan

Editing and page layout by Cambridge Publishing Management Ltd,
Unit 2, Burr Elm Court, Caldecote CB23 7NU
Series Editor: Karen Beaulah

Published by Thomas Cook Publishing
A division of Thomas Cook Tour Operations Ltd
Company Registration No. 1450464 England

PO Box 227, The Thomas Cook Business Park,
Coningsby Road, Peterborough PE3 8SB, United Kingdom
E-mail: books@thomascook.com
www.thomascookpublishing.com
Tel: +44 (0)1733 416477

ISBN: 978-1-84157-820-0

Text © 2007 Thomas Cook Publishing
Maps © 2007 Thomas Cook Publishing

Project Editor: Sasha Heseltine
Production/DTP Editor: Steven Collins

Printed and bound in Italy by: Printer Trento.

Front cover credits, L–R: © Schmid Reinhard/Simephoto-4Corners Images;
© Bildagentur Huber/Giovanni/4Corners Images; © Bildagentur
Huber/Giovanni/4Corners Images
Back cover credits, L–R: © Giovanni Simeone/4Corners Images; © Darrell
Gulin/Getty Images

Contents

Introduction

Costa Rica is a unique country to visit; spectacular natural scenery, an abundance of wildlife and a well-earned reputation for peacefulness make it a haven in many ways. Due to the country's small size it is possible to make a lot of a relatively short trip, although there is plenty to occupy visitors who choose to stay longer.

In fact there is such astonishing variety to the landscape that there is always more to explore. Simmering volcanoes and lofty mountain peaks loom large over fertile valleys, while at the coasts tropical rainforests stretch down to sandy beaches. With this diversity of habitats comes a diversity of occupants, from tiny hummingbirds to big cats (although the latter are significantly more elusive than the former). Monkeys spring through the rainforest canopy, crocodiles sun themselves on river banks, turtles nest on beaches and sloths cling to tree trunks. Costa Rica has some of the greatest biodiversity in the world and it has earned wide acclaim for safeguarding this natural legacy with a network of protected areas covering more than 25 per cent of the country. The situation is not completely idyllic; many species are endangered and deforestation and overdevelopment are threatening some areas. However, Costa Rica has created a positive model for combining tourism and ecology, attracting everyone from wildlife enthusiasts to surfers. Tourism is now the main industry in Costa Rica and an estimated 1.6 million people visit each year.

The country particularly excels in offering a taste of outdoor adventure with a selection of activities to tempt visitors of all ages and inclinations. Action-packed days can include hiking through the rainforest, abseiling down waterfalls, kayaking in the watery world of Tortuguero or riding around the northern plains on horseback. The more relaxing options include taking a stroll around a coffee plantation, joining a catamaran sailing trip or simply chilling on a gorgeous beach. Although stunning natural beauty and wildlife are Costa Rica's main tourist attractions, the country is also renowned for its long-standing serenity and stability in a region generally characterised by volatility. The nation has been a democracy since the late 19th century, but 1949 was a particularly important year, when universal suffrage was brought in and the army was abolished.

Modern Costa Rica is a peaceful nation known for the friendliness of its people, although it is not without social difficulties, including significant poverty and massive debt. Still, the standard of living in Costa Rica is one of the highest in Latin America and the overall picture, particularly in terms of health and education, is positive. Life expectancy is estimated at 77 and the adult literacy rate stands at 96 per cent. Costa Ricans – or Ticos (Ticas for women) as they call themselves – are proud of their country and welcoming to visitors, an attitude neatly summed up by the national catch phrase, *pura vida* (pure life).

A red-eyed tree frog from Costa Rica's rainforests

The land

The Republic of Costa Rica lies towards the south of the Central American isthmus, bordering Nicaragua to the north and Panama to the south. To the west is the Pacific, to the east the Caribbean. Although Costa Rica covers a landmass of just 51,100sq km (1,972sq miles), there is an amazing diversity of ecosystems packed into the country's borders, from active volcanoes and misty cloud forests to tropical rainforests and coastal mangrove swamps.

Climate

Costa Rica is a subtropical country where the sun rises at around 6am and sets at around 6pm throughout the year. The seasons can broadly be divided into dry (December to April), known locally as *verano* (summer), and wet (May to November), known as *invierno* (winter) and also more pleasantly as the 'green season'. However, there are striking variations in weather throughout this small country. The warm, humid Caribbean and southern Pacific coasts receive relatively high rainfall even in the dry season and are drenched in the wet season. By contrast, it gets extremely dry and hot in the northwest, while San José and the central valley experience gentle warmth year round and in the highlands it even gets cold. Temperatures vary from over 35°C (95°F) in the northwestern dry season to below 0°C (32°F) on the highest peaks; but the one thing that is consistent throughout Costa Rica is the strong sun.

Landscape

Mountain ranges, peppered with volcanoes and cloud forests, run the length of Costa Rica from northwest to south, forming a natural divide between the country's western and eastern sides. San José and several of the country's main cities are situated in the agricultural Valle Central (Central Valley), which lies in the heart of the highlands and is home to more than half of Costa Rica's population. Travelling through the pretty countryside of the Central Valley and sloping highland peaks, an area also known as the Meseta Central (or Central Plateau), it is hard to believe that you are in a tropical country. The highest mountain summits are found near the border with Panama and the tallest of them all, at 3,820m (12,533ft), is Cerro Chirripó. The Pacific coastline, measuring 1,245km (774 miles), encompasses a great variety of landscapes. The open plains and dry forests of the north give way to the

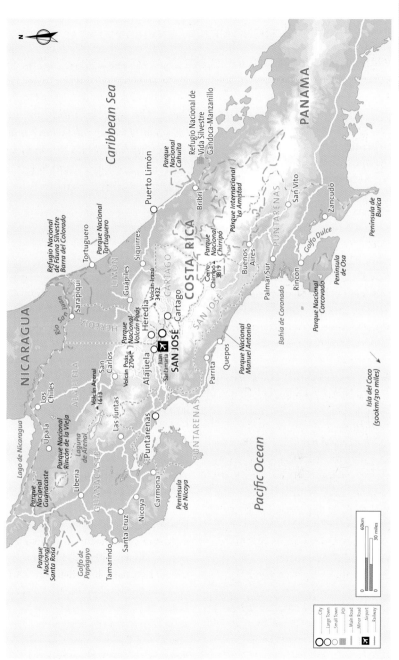

tropical rainforests of the south, via surf-washed beaches. By contrast the Caribbean coastline, only 212km (132 miles) long, is characterised by verdant, humid lagoons, swamps and waterways. About 25 per cent of Costa Rica's territory is protected within national parks, refuges and reserves, which have been established over the last 30 years or so.

Forests

Costa Rica is host to five main types of forest, with a dazzling variety of plants and wildlife between them. Sadly, however, deforestation is a major issue with most of the forest outside the national park system having been cleared. The lush, evergreen tropical rainforest has the greatest diversity,

An aerial view of the rainforest highlights the density of the tree canopy

ENVIRONMENTAL FACTS

- All energy needs (except oil for transportation) met through renewable sources (hydroelectric dams and wind farms)
- More than a quarter of total territory (nearly 1.2 million ha/2.9 million acres) protected in national parks, wildlife refuges and biological reserves.
- Greater relative biodiversity than any other country on Earth, with 615 species of flora and fauna per 10,000sq km (3,860sq miles).
- Home to 205 species of mammals (half of which are bats), over 830 species of birds (twice as many as the USA and Canada combined), over 400 species of reptiles and amphibians, 560 species of butterflies (more than in Africa).
- Twelve distinct climatic regions, all in a country the size of Wales.

with more than 500 species of tree. Corcovado National Park protects the last sizeable area of rainforest on the Pacific coast of Central America. The tropical dry forest found in the Guanacaste region consists mainly of deciduous or semi-deciduous trees, and is subject to dramatic seasonal changes. This is the most endangered of the forest types because of deforestation and climate change. On the high slopes of Costa Rica's mountains, premontane wet forests are found, giving way to tropical montane rainforest at the highest altitudes. This can be seen at Poás and Irazú volcanoes and is also known as dwarf forest because of the shrunken look of the vegetation. Finally, and possibly most famously, there are the tropical lower montane

Pacific coast beaches are often fringed by tropical forests

cloud forests, such as Monteverde. This enchanting and unique environment is formed by mists creating a constant and almost total humidity.

Coastline and wetlands

Costa Rica's two coastlines are so different from each other that they feel like different countries. The Caribbean coast is sunny but never without rain for long, particularly the northern half. It is a land of canals, mangrove swamps and river deltas, home to turtles, crocodiles and caimans among many other animals. The Tortuguero area of the northern Caribbean, where dense coastal rainforest is infiltrated by a network of waterways, has been described as Costa Rica's mini-Amazon.

The southern Caribbean coast has some of the most stunning beaches, as well as endangered coral reefs within protected areas. The Pacific coast is characterised by its beautiful black- and white-sand beaches, often fringed by tropical forests. The rugged Nicoya peninsula encompasses several coastal nature reserves, with abundant marine life. The Pacific coast also contains the largest mangrove estuary in Latin America, which is protected. Like the coral reefs of the Caribbean and the southern Pacific, mangrove swamps are a delicate and endangered habitat. Another reason for the safeguarding of coastal areas is that many are nesting sites for sea turtles, including the highly endangered leatherbacks.

History

Relatively little is known about pre-Columbian history in Costa Rica, although human habitation can be traced back to 1000 BC. As a Spanish colony Costa Rica was virtually ignored by the empire, but after independence it went on to become the most prosperous country in Central America. Although there were periods of war and political difficulty during the 19th and 20th centuries, the modern Republic of Costa Rica is a stable democracy.

1000 BC　City of Guayabo established. It is estimated that the site was home to a population of 10,000 at its peak.

AD 1400　Guayabo is abandoned – it is not known why.

1502　Christopher Columbus arrives near Limón on 18 September, on his fourth and final voyage to the Americas. The indigenous population of the area that is now Costa Rica is divided into chiefdoms, separate from each other and with their own distinctive cultures.

1522　Spanish Captain Gil González Dávila is inspired by the golden bands worn by some of the native people in their noses and ears to name the country Costa Rica (Rich Coast). However, Costa Rica proves a difficult country to colonise and the Spanish are more interested in other countries of the Americas.

1563　Cartago is established as the colonial capital by Juan Vásquez de Coronado. Tragically, many of the indigenous peoples perish from European diseases brought in by the

Pre-Columbian artefacts at the National Museum in San José

Spaniards, while others flee to the highlands.

1564–1821 Costa Rica remains one of the least regarded outposts in the Spanish empire, isolated from the colonial centres and trading routes. It experiences less wealth, but also less turmoil, than other colonies. Although slavery exists, the landowners are relatively poor themselves and have to farm their own land, so the social divide is not as great as it is elsewhere.

1737 San José is founded, although Cartago is still the capital.

1821 The Central American nations declare independence from Spain. The day of independence is 15 September, but the news reaches the inhabitants of Costa Rica a month later.

1823 There is a brief civil war between the cities of San José and Alajuela, who want to join a new confederation of Central American states, and those of Cartago and Heredia, who are for joining Mexico. San José and Alajuela win and San José becomes the capital city.

1824 Juan Mora Fernandez is elected as the first head of state. Under his administration, infrastructure, public education and coffee production in Costa Rica are developed and the country thrives. Over the following century the coffee trade will lead it to become wealthier than its Central American neighbours.

1855–6 An American adventurer called William Walker arrives in Costa Rica with a group of followers. They plan to enslave the whole of Central America. Juan Rafael Mora, Costa Rica's current president, gathers 9,000 civilians and they defeat Walker at the battle of Santa Rosa. A drummer boy named Juan Santamaría is remembered as a hero for his part in the victory.

1860–89 Costa Rica makes the transition to full democracy, although this is problematic at times with ongoing power struggles and only the rich deciding the outcome of elections. Free, compulsory primary education is established in 1869, although families in remote areas are unable to access this, and progress is made in taxation for public projects and in military policy.

1889 The first democratic elections are held, but women and the country's black minority are not allowed to vote.

1917 There is a brief lapse in democracy when Federico Tinoco overthrows the president and forms a dictatorship, but his regime lasts only a year before he is forced to flee to Europe.

1940 Rafael Angel Calderón Guardia is elected and introduces reforms including minimum-wage laws and an eight-hour work day.

1948 Civil war erupts after Calderón refuses to accept that he has not been re-elected. The opposition to his false presidency is led by José (Don Pepe) Figueres Ferrer.

More than 2,000 people are killed before Figueres wins the war. He governs for 18 months and then hands over to the elected president Otilio Ulate.

1949 The modern Costa Rican constitution is formed. The army is abolished and Costa Rica begins to establish its current reputation for democracy, peace and stability.

1971 Parque Nacional Santa Rosa, Costa Rica's first national park, is established.

1987 Oscar Arias Sánchez of the PLN (National Liberation Party), president since 1986, is awarded the Nobel Peace Prize for his efforts to promote peace in Central America.

1990–2006 Costa Rican politics are dominated by the PUSC (Social Christian Unity Party), who win three out of the next four general elections.

2006 Oscar Arias is re-elected president 16 years after the end of his first term.

José (Don Pepe) Figueres Ferrer (1906–1990)

Politics

The Republic of Costa Rica began a progression towards democracy soon after gaining independence from Spain, but the modern political system really dates to the constitution of 1949. It was at this point that the foundation for the stability, peace and high regard for human rights and social welfare the nation enjoys today was cemented. At the time of writing, Oscar Arias Sánchez is president and head of state, having narrowly triumphed over competitor Ottón Solís in the closest-run election in modern Costa Rican history. One of the most pressing issues currently being debated is whether the country should join the Central American Free Trade Agreement (CAFTA). Supporters of the treaty cite the potential economic benefits, while critics state concerns that small businesses and the environment would suffer.

The modern Costa Rican constitution

The constitution was drawn up in 1949 and one of the many significant changes it heralded was the abolition of the armed forces, a powerful symbol of peace following the bloodshed of the civil war the previous year. Social security and social assistance were also introduced, the banking system was nationalised and the progressive education and health reforms brought in previously were expanded. Universal suffrage was achieved as women and black Costa Ricans were given the vote and voting was made mandatory for citizens over 18. Although compulsory voting is not enforced, Costa Rica generally has a relatively good election turnout. Elections are held every four years and voters choose a president and two vice presidents, who then serve a single term in office. The constitution prevents presidents and the deputies of the 57-member Legislative Assembly from running for successive terms. Costa Rica has an

Children demonstrate to demand a new school

Bellavista Fortress bears the scars of the civil war in 1948

indicate that the ascendancy of the two main parties is waning slightly.

Political trends

In politics, as in many other aspects of Costa Rican life, the family plays a key role and elections can seem like a festive occasion. Families will often remain loyal to a political party over generations and at election time many voters display the colours of their chosen party on banners or shirts. This tendency towards family tradition has also more directly influenced the governance of the country. During the 1990s the sons of Rafael Angel Calderón Guardia (PUSC) and Don Pepe Figueres Ferrer (PLN) each served a presidential term. They were not the first to follow in paternal footsteps, as 33 out of the 44 presidents before 1970 were descended from three of the country's original colonisers.

independent judiciary, with a Supreme Court of Justice comprising 22 magistrates who serve eight-year terms, which can be renewed.

The political parties

Of Costa Rica's many political parties, the Partido de Liberación Nacional (PLN: National Liberation Party) and the Partido de Unidad Social Cristiana (PUSC: Social Christian Unity Party) have been the dominant players since the 1940s. The PLN, led by current president Oscar Arias Sánchez, is inclined slightly to the social left, while the PUSC leans to the Christian right, but both parties are essentially centrist. A number of minority parties hold a significant total of seats in the Legislative Assembly between them. They have been gaining some ground in recent years as the gap between lead presidential candidates has become increasingly slim, which would seem to

THE ABOLITION OF THE ARMY

When the armed forces were abolished in the constitution of 1949 it was an historic decision; Costa Rica was the first country in the world to take such a step. The man in charge, acting president José 'Don Pepe' Figueres Ferrer, was motivated by a desire to curb any future political instability of the kind which had so recently erupted and which had long plagued the country's neighbours. He also saw it as a way to preserve resources. To this day Costa Rica still has no army, although there is a powerful police force, and the stability Figueres hoped for has been well maintained. However, a few active paramilitary groups have been the cause of some disquiet.

Culture

Costa Rica has not benefited from the same kind of rich cultural legacy as many of its neighbours. The small indigenous population was dramatically reduced at the time of colonisation, so there was no significant development of traditional arts and crafts. Other art forms were also historically neglected because of the country's poverty and relative social uneventfulness. However, as Costa Rica has developed so has its culture, and in recent years the arts have begun to thrive.

People and community

The vast majority of Costa Rica's population of four million is *mestizo*, of mixed Spanish and Indian and/or black descent. The minority is made up of

A Costa Rican 'Tico'

indigenous Costa Ricans (just 1 per cent), black descendants of Jamaican immigrants (3 per cent), Chinese immigrants (1 per cent) and a few others. There are also a significant number of resident Nicaraguans who have moved across the border in search of jobs, and on the opposite end of the wealth spectrum, expatriate North Americans drawn to the charms of a tropical paradise. Just as the landscape varies greatly throughout the country, so do the customs and traditions of the people. Most black Costa Ricans live on the Caribbean coast and have a distinctive culture which incorporates their Jamaican heritage. People in Guanacaste also have a characteristic culture which sets them apart. More than three-quarters of Ticos are Catholic, but many go to church only on holidays and for the sacraments. The family is accorded great social importance and cultural celebrations generally have a family focus.

Indigenous groups

The small indigenous population of Costa Rica, which consists of a number of distinct groups, was completely marginalised from the rest of society for hundreds of years. From the mid-20th century the government began to recognise this and indigenous people were finally given citizenship rights. However, they still face a unique set of problems, many stemming from isolation and land disputes. Today, some native Costa Ricans have integrated with the general population, while others live in designated self-governing reserves. These communities mainly live off the land, but in recent years many have begun to make traditional craft items for sale. They have retained, to a varying degree, their traditional customs and languages while also speaking Spanish and

Indigenous people on the Maleku Reserve demonstrate a typical dance

adopting some aspects of modern Costa Rican life. Interest in indigenous cultures, folklore and artisan traditions is increasing, both among visitors to the country and in local universities. Pre-Columbian artefacts are on display in San José's museums, and some towns, such as Guaitil on the Nicoya Peninsula, focus on the production of ceramics and other craft items inspired by indigenous traditions.

Art and crafts

Artistic activities really began to progress in Costa Rica in the early 20th century. In the late 1920s a group of painters called the Group of New Sensibility developed the country's first individual style, known as the 'landscape' movement. This group included Teodorico Quiros, who was much later given an award for lifetime achievement in the 'creation and

INDIGENOUS RESERVATIONS

In 1977 the government established 22 reservations (many of them in the south) to enable indigenous people to live in self-governing communities. This marked a step in the right direction in terms of safeguarding native cultures. However, problems persist and there seems to be a double-edged sword of isolation, poverty and land infringements on reserves against loss of culture if people do decide to integrate more. Many indigenous communities welcome visitors who are interested in learning about their cultures and buying traditional craft items. Contact the organisation ATEC (*see p129*) if you are in southern Costa Rica and would like to visit a reserve.

A potter at work

promotion of Costa Rican artistic culture'. Costa Rica's most internationally renowned sculptor, Francisco Zuñiga, created huge statues of the female figure during a long career beginning in the 1930s. As the 20th century advanced various distinct styles followed these early examples. Modern artists produce work across the visual arts spectrum and, although not well known internationally, they are starting to gain recognition. San José is the headquarters of the art scene, with the majority of the country's museums and galleries. Since 1992, the capital has also hosted the biannual International Art Festival.

Costa Rican crafts have experienced a revival recently, initiated by the demand generated by the growing tourist industry. Although many of the creations are identikit, there are some skilful and interesting crafts being made. The woodwork of Escazú and the ceramics of Santa Ana, both in the highlands, are examples of this, while a traditional pottery business is thriving in Guanacaste. However, the Costa Rican capital of crafts is the village of Sarchí, famous for its brightly decorated *carretas* (ox-carts).

Theatre

Performance art has been a cultural success story for Costa Rica, as an exploration of the many theatres in San José reveals. Costa Ricans have long loved theatre, and drama has been taught at schools since the beginning of the 20th century. The famous Teatro Nacional (National Theatre), built in 1897, is an important venue for an array of performances including plays, opera and poetry readings. Going to the theatre is an enjoyable, affordable and highly varied experience, popular with both Ticos and tourists. Most productions are in Spanish, but they can be fun even if you do not understand much of the language. The Little Theatre Group (*see p34*) performs plays in English.

Music and dance

Music and dancing are integral elements of Costa Rican culture, and styles reflect the varied heritage of the population. Young Ticos like to listen to Western pop and rock songs, but they like to dance to the evocative rhythms of Latin, particularly *salsa* and *merengue*, and Caribbean music. Live music is also popular in a selection of venues. In Guanacaste the tradition of folkloric music and dancing still exists, and the official national dance is called the Punto Guanacasteco. *Marimba* (xylophone) music, which has African roots, is found in Costa Rica as elsewhere in the isthmus. Guitars are typically used for folk dancing, and

traditional pre-Columbian instruments such as the *chirimia* (oboe) are still played to complement some Chorotega dances. Since the 1970s a tradition of South American-style *peñas* (acoustic folk songs) has also developed in Costa Rica. The Caribbean coast is different from the rest of the country in music and dance as in many things, with its Afro-Caribbean influenced culture of calypso and reggae.

Inside San José's Teatro Nacional

Festivals and events

Many of the festivals celebrated in Costa Rica are linked to Catholicism and they are generally lively affairs. Wherever you are staying, there is sure to be a fiesta nearby with music, food and dancing. It's a great way to meet the locals and join in with town and village events.

January

Fiesta de Santa Cruz (mid-January) Religious procession and activities including folk dancing, Costa Rican-style bull fighting, rodeo and a beauty pageant in Santa Cruz de Nicoya.

Fiesta de los Diablitos (Festival of the Little Devils, 31 December–2 January in Boruca, 5–8 February in Curré) An indigenous festival, during which the fight between the Indians and the Spanish is re-created with dances and colourful wooden masks, with one difference – the Spaniards lose.

February

Puntarenas Carnival (last week of February) Carnival parades, music and fireworks.

March

Día de los Boyeros (Oxcart Drivers' Day, second Sunday in March) A parade of oxcarts in Escazú held in honour of the drivers.

Día de San José (St Joseph's Day, 19th) Fairs, church services and parades take place to honour the patron saint of the capital.

Festival de Arte (Festival of the Arts) Takes place for two weeks in March every even year.

Semana Santa (Holy Week) The week preceding Easter weekend. The Thursday and Friday are the official holidays, but the whole country virtually shuts down from Holy Thursday to Easter Monday.

April

Día de Juan Santamaría (11th) Official country holiday commemorating the national hero. The celebrations, with marching bands, parades, concerts and dances, actually last a week.

Semana Santa (*see above*).

May

Día de los Trabajadores (Labour Day, 1st) The president delivers his annual 'state of the nation' address on a country holiday.

July

Fiesta de La Virgen del Mar (Festival of the Virgin of the Sea, Saturday closest to 16th) This celebration is held in Puntarenas and Playa del Coco, with colourful regattas of decorated boats and activities including parades, concerts and fireworks.

Día de Guanacaste (Guanacaste Day, 25th) Celebrations are held to mark the annexation of Guanacaste from Nicaragua in 1824.

August

Virgen de los Angeles (2nd) The patron saint of Costa Rica, La Negrita, is honoured with a pilgrimage from San José to Cartago.

September

Independence Day (15th) Parades and parties throughout Costa Rica celebrate the Central American countries' independence from Spain in 1821. There is a student relay race across the Central American isthmus carrying a 'freedom torch', which arrives in Cartago at 6pm.

October

Día de la Raza Carnival (Day of the People, 12th) The Limón Carnival celebrates Columbus's arrival in the New World during the week before 12 October. It is a week of partying, with Afro-Caribbean dance and costumes, calypso music, children's activities and fireworks.

November

Día de los Muertos (All Souls' Day, 2nd) Official national holiday. Families visit cemeteries to pay their respects and place flowers on graves.

December

La Inmaculada Concepción (Immaculate Conception, 8th) An important religious holiday nationwide. In the Indian village of Boruca an ancient Indian ritual is combined with this festival into the Fiesta de los Negritos.

Christmas and end of year celebrations Celebrations begin in early December. *Portales* (nativity scenes) are displayed and houses are decorated. The weeks either side of Christmas Day are particularly celebrated, with carnival and horse parades, fireworks and, bizarrely, copious amounts of 'snow' confetti. Christmas Day is family-oriented. Apples and grapes are some of the main festive foods.

Fireworks during the December 'Festival de la Luz'

Highlights

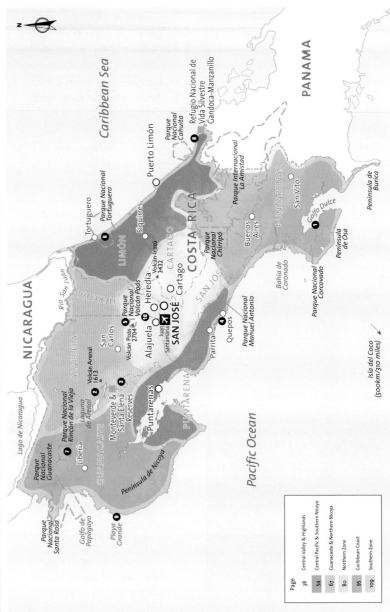

N

Caribbean Sea

PANAMA

Refugio Nacional de
Vida Silvestre
Gandoca-Manzanillo

Parque
Nacional
Cahuita

Puerto Limón

Tortuguero

Parque Nacional
Tortuguero

Parque Internacional
La Amistad

LIMÓN

Siquirres

San Vito

PUNTARENAS

Golfo Dulce

Peninsula de
Burica

CARTAGO

Volcán Irazú
3432

COSTA RICA

Parque
Nacional
Chirripó

Buenos
Aires

Rio San Juan

HEREDIA

Heredia

Parque
Nacional
Volcán Poás

Cartago

SAN JOSÉ

Peninsula
de Osa

NICARAGUA

San
Carlos

Volcán Poás
2704

Alajuela

Juan
Santamaría

SAN JOSÉ

Bahía de
Coronado

Parque Nacional
Corcovado

ALAJUELA

Volcán Arenal
1613

Laguna
de Arenal

Parrita

Quepos

Parque Nacional
Manuel Antonio

Monteverde &
Santa Elena
Reserves

Puntarenas

PUNTARENAS

Lago de Nicaragua

Parque Nacional
Rincón de la Vieja

Liberia

GUANACASTE

Peninsula de Nicoya

Pacific Ocean

Isla del Coco
(500km/310 miles)

Parque
Nacional
Guanacaste

Golfo de
Papagayo

Parque
Nacional
Santa Rosa

Playa
Grande

Page	
38	Central Valley & Highlands
54	Central Pacific & Southern Nicoya
67	Guanacaste & Northern Nicoya
80	Northern Zone
95	Caribbean Coast
109	Southern Zone

1 Peninsula de Osa and Golfo Dulce
Enjoying the tropical haven of one of Costa Rica's most beautiful and remote spots, where pastimes include trekking through lush rainforest, kayaking along the coast and watching the sun set on palm-fringed beaches (*see p116*).

2 Volcán Arenal and Laguna de Arenal Admiring the dramatic spectacle of one of the world's most active volcanoes and sampling some of the water sports and outdoor adventures on offer in the surrounding area (*see p90*).

3 Cloud forest reserves of Monteverde and Santa Elena
Hiking through an ethereal forest where the trees are shrouded in layers of dense vegetation, and catching glimpses of colourful, exotic birds through the mist (*see p81*).

4 Parque Nacional Manuel Antonio
Strolling along idyllic coconut-speckled beaches and through coastal rainforest at one of the most popular national parks (*see p58*).

5 Parque Nacional Volcán Poás
Gazing into the active crater of easily accessible Poás volcano, the steaming centrepiece of a park which also features dwarf cloud forest and a sparkling lake in an old crater (*see p46*).

6 Parque Nacional Tortuguero
Spotting wildlife on a boat trip through otherwise inaccessible jungle and experiencing the vibrant culture of Costa Rica's Caribbean coast (*see p98*).

7 Parque Nacional Rincón de la Vieja Exploring a mystical volcanic landscape with trails past bubbling mud pots and geysers, before treating tired muscles to a soak in a hot spring (*see p71*).

8 Refugio Nacional de Vida Silvestre Gandoca-Manzanillo
Relaxing on Manzanillo beach, widely considered one of the most scenic in the country, and exploring the pristine coastline and wildlife protected by Gandoca-Manzanillo reserve (*see p102*).

9 Parque Nacional Marino Las Baulas Witnessing the touching natural spectacle of turtle nesting, combined with a beach break on one of the beautiful beaches for which this part of the country is renowned (*see pp69–70*).

10 Central Valley coffee Enjoying the country's favourite drink at one of the panoramic coffee plantations in the verdant Central Valley (*see p50*).

Suggested itineraries

Long weekend

Make the most of a brief stay by heading straight for one of the national parks.

Guanacaste

Spend a day hiking through tropical dry forest around an active volcano in **Parque Nacional Rincón de la Vieja**. From this elevation you can admire a panoramic vista of the Nicoya Peninsula before winding your way down to Playa Tamarindo for a couple of days of sun, sand and surf. Make the most of your short break with an excursion to the mangroves of Tamarindo estuary, a night tour at the turtle nesting **Playa Grande** or a snorkelling trip. Travel by car or tourist bus (*see p132*).

Rainforest retreat

The tropical paradise of the **Península de Osa and Golfo Dulce** is the perfect place to drift away from reality for a few days. Fly into San José's international airport, then straight out of the capital again on a domestic flight to Puerto Jimenéz or Golfito. From here it will be just a short drive or boat ride to a coastal rainforest lodge (*see p136*).

Retreat to a hammock at Golfo Dulce

The backwaters of Tortuguero National Park

One week

With a week at your disposal you can combine a couple of different attractions and get a feel for the contrasts in landscape which make Costa Rica such a fascinating country.

Northern highlights

This is one of Costa Rica's most adventure travel-oriented regions. Start by visiting the fascinating cloud forests of **Monteverde and Santa Elena**. Continue your trip with a bumpy ride to the town of La Fortuna, a journey which feels like an adventure in itself, especially if you incorporate a horse ride for part of the way (*see p149*). The expansive Laguna de Arenal offers great windsurfing, and highly active **Volcán Arenal**, which towers over the region, is a particularly impressive sight. Hike around the base of the volcano or to nearby waterfalls or try white-water rafting or kayaking. Then, head east for a hot-air balloon ride at Muelle de San Carlos (*see p171*) or a leisurely boat ride to Caño Negro wildlife reserve (*see pp92–3*).

Culture and Caribbean

Spend your first day exploring the capital (*see p32* in San José chapter for a suggested walk) and your second branching out into the picturesque rolling hills of the Central Valley region. This trip is best done by car (if you are not driving there are tour companies which offer a driver-guide service, *see p133*). Visit Guayabo monument (*see p43*), making a detour to the old capital of Cartago and for a picnic stop in the pretty Orosí valley (*see p52*). On the third day, travel to **Parque Nacional Tortuguero** on a scenic journey by road and river. Many of the lodges in Tortuguero include a return trip from San José in their prices (*see p136*). The wildlife-rich watery wonderland of Tortuguero will keep you occupied for several days. On your last day, based back in the capital, visit a Central Valley **coffee plantation** and **Volcán Poás**.

Two weeks

Two weeks is long enough to travel across the country, taking in a variety of beautiful areas and trying out different activities.

Volcanoes and forests

Set off from San José to **Arenal** volcano for a smoking introduction to Costa Rica and spend a couple of days exploring the area. Continue on to **Monteverde and Santa Elena** on the Lake Trail (*see p90*). Then take a bus to **Rincón de la Vieja**. Interbus (*see p132*) offers this route. Take a transfer bus or taxi (ask at your hotel) to Liberia (*see p68*), where you could hire a car to wind your way back to the capital on the Interamericana road or hop on a bus and sit back to enjoy the Guanacaste scenery and Pacific views.

To break your journey at the end of this action-packed first week, stay two nights in San José and spend a day visiting easily accessible Volcán Poás and enjoying the refreshing climate of the lush Central Valley. For a memorable conclusion to your holiday, travel down to the remote **Península de Osa**. The drive is long, but scenic and straightforward, as the Interamericana goes almost all the way. Alternatively, take a short plane ride (*see p133*). You should have three or four days to spend exploring the classic tropical rainforest of the Osa region.

Coast to coast

Manuel Antonio is easily reached from San José by car or bus. For a gentle introduction to the tropical rainforest, spend your first day here (making sure this is not a Monday, when the park is closed) strolling along gorgeous beaches and well-maintained forest

Volcán Arenal near San José

trails. Continue your exploration of the Central Pacific region by heading for **Parque Nacional Carara** (*see p57*). This short journey can be done by bus (take the bus route towards Puntarenas and ask to be dropped off at Carara), car or on an organised day tour from Manuel Antonio. Try and stop by the Río Tárcoles where you may well see a number of crocodiles basking in the hot sun. For a relaxing third day in the region, try an ocean or river boat trip (ask at your hotel). Traverse the country via San José and stop off for a day, visiting a **coffee plantation** for a change of scene from the tropical coasts. If not driving, take a bus from the capital to Cahuita village, from where you can explore the national park of the same name, before continuing a little further south to **Gandoca-Manzanillo** wildlife refuge. You will see some of the most stunning beaches in the country along the southern Caribbean coast. Finally, double back and head north to Moín, near Puerto Limón, to catch a boat to **Tortuguero**. You will probably need to spend a night near Moín as boats generally leave in the morning.

Longer – the essence of Costa Rica

Lucky you! With more than two weeks to spend you will be able to incorporate many of the most distinctive places scattered around the country. Think about combining a couple of the itineraries outlined above and adding some extra stops along the way. For example, start with the 'Rainforest retreat' then drive from Golfito to the town of San Isidro de el General (*see p120*), from where you could either spend some time exploring the mountains of the Cordillera de Talamanca, or head down to the coast to Parque Nacional Marino Ballena (*see p110*). Continue on to San José to start the 'Culture and Caribbean' itinerary, adding an extra day in the Central Valley to visit Poás volcano, La Paz waterfall gardens and the Doka Estate coffee plantation. Another suggestion is to lengthen the 'volcanoes and forests' itinerary by incorporating one of the Guanacaste beaches and Parque Nacional Palo Verde. You could also add extra time in the Northern Zone at the beginning for some adventure activities and extra time in the Southern Zone at the end to visit an indigenous reserve or hike through Parque Nacional Corcovado (*see p114*).

The Manuel Antonio National Park on the west coast of Costa Rica

San José

Costa Rica's bustling capital and only sizeable city is not an established city-break destination, more usually a stopping-off point en route to the natural attractions of the countryside. In many ways San José seems to be at odds with the rest of the country, a broad urban sprawl that contrasts sharply with its beautiful setting. However, there is interest to be found here, from its eventful history to its vibrant and cosmopolitan atmosphere.

See pp32–3 for walk route.

San José assumed capital status from Cartago in 1823 following a battle and then had to fight off the combined forces of Cartago, Heredia and Alajuela 13 years later in order to retain that status. In the mid-20th century a process of rapid expansion saw San José spread across the Central Valley to become the city it is today, home to more than a third of the population. Sadly, with the economic growth came increased crime and poverty, which, along with the sheer volume and speed of traffic, contribute to a feeling that being a pedestrian is not ideal. Certainly, it is advisable to take safety

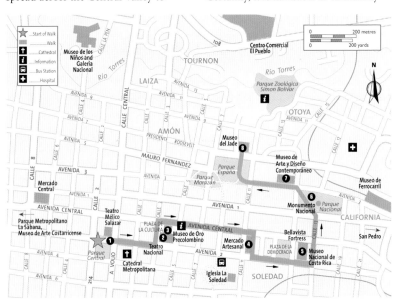

precautions such as avoiding walking at night and not carrying or wearing expensive items or any more money than you need.

On a more positive note, however, central San José is easily accessible and navigable by foot, with an impressive range of cultural attractions gathered in a small area. Add to this the colourful markets, array of international restaurants and lively festivals, and there is plenty to occupy visitors.

Aerial view of San José

Museums and galleries

Costa Rica may be primarily a nature destination, but San José has a wide variety of museums and galleries to interest those who are also looking to spend some time learning about the culture of the country and region. Several of these museums are inventively housed in sites originally built for very different purposes; most notably, the Children's Museum is located inside an old prison, while the National Museum occupies the historic Bellavista Fortress, the headquarters of the army before it was abolished.

Museo de Arte Costarricense

The Costa Rican Art Museum, which displays 19th- and 20th-century works, has one of the prettiest settings of San José's museums. Continuing the tradition of recycling buildings, it is based in a colonial-style building that used to be an airport, in La Sabana Park, next to an open-air sculpture garden.

Parque La Sabana. Tel: (506) 222 7155. www.musarco.go.cr. Open: Tue–Sun 10am–4pm. Admission charge (free on Sun).

Museo de Arte y Diseño Contemporáneo

On the eastern edge of the Parque España is an old factory building, which has been creatively transformed into an arts complex. This is the home of the Centro Nacional de la Cultura, Juventud y Deportes (Ministry of Culture, Youth and Sports) or CENAC. The development also includes two theatres, an open-air amphitheatre and a dance studio, but for modern art enthusiasts the Museum of Contemporary Art and Design is the main attraction. It displays work by Central American artists working in a variety of styles.

Av 3, Calle 13–15. Tel: (506) 257 7202. www.madc.ac.cr. Open: Tue–Sat 10am–5pm. Admission charge.

The Barrio Amón district, home to many of the city's museums

Museo del Jade

The Jade Museum provides a fascinating glimpse of pre-Columbian culture both in Costa Rica and throughout Central America. Intriguingly, none of the jade was extracted in the country, so the discovery of these artefacts is evidence of interaction between the indigenous peoples of the isthmus. Alongside the beautifully crafted and multicoloured jade jewellery and objects on display there are also artefacts made from other materials, including some intricate stone statues. All the objects held some symbolic significance in pre-Columbian society, for example as an indication of status or as magic stones used in rituals.
Instituto Nacional de Seguros, Av 7–9, Calle 9–11. Tel: (506) 287 6034. www.ins-cr.com. Open: Mon–Fri 8.30am–3.30pm. Admission charge (children under 12 free).

Museo Nacional de Costa Rica

The National Museum was established in 1887, making it very old by Costa

Rican standards, and it occupied several different sites before coming to rest in the Bellavista ('Good View') Fortress – a building with an interesting history. It was the headquarters of the army, until its 1949 abolition, which President José Figueres announced at the fortress. Inside the museum is a series of exhibitions about archaeology, history and natural history. Information is displayed in English as well as Spanish and provides an absorbing, and at times disturbing, outline of Costa Rica's history. Some of the collections provide an intriguing insight into the culture of indigenous peoples, both past and present. These include gold jewellery which was used to indicate status and stone tables whose purposes varied from the sacrificial to the culinary.
Calle 17, Av Central–2. Tel: (506) 257 1433. www.museocostarica.go.cr. Open: Tue–Sat 8.30am–4.30pm, Sun 9.00am–4.30pm. Admission charge (child/student discount).

Museo de los Niños and Galería Nacional

Perhaps most intriguing of the building and museum pairings is the location of the Centro de el Ciencia y la Cultura (Science and Culture Centre) in an old prison. The interactive Children's Museum is the biggest attraction in the complex, which also houses a small museum dedicated to the history of the country's penitentiary system, and the National Gallery, which

uses some of the old cells as a display space for modern art.
North end of Calle 4. Tel: (506) 258 4929. www.museocr.com. Open: Tue–Fri 8am–3.30pm, Sat & Sun 9.30am–4.30pm. Admission charge for Children's Museum, Gallery free.

Museo de Oro Precolombino

The popular Pre-Columbian Gold Museum displays one of the largest collections of pre-Columbian gold artefacts, an impressive achievement for a country where such artefacts are relatively scarce. Many of the gold pieces are delicately ornate renderings of evil spirits in animal form, such as birds of prey, jaguars and frogs. They were predominantly made by the Diquis, who lived in the southwest region of the country. For anyone with an interest in the culture of Costa Rica's ancient indigenous people, as well as for those with magpie tendencies, the shiny collection of the Gold Museum is worth a visit.
Basement, Plaza de la Cultura. Tel: (506) 243 4202. www.museosdelbancocentral.org. Open: Tue–Sun 10am–5pm. Admission charge.

Artefact in the Pre-Columbian Gold Museum

Walk: The cultural centre, San José

The roads in San José are easy to navigate, as they are numbered in a logical grid system (east–west avenidas (avenues) and north–south calles (streets)). This city-centre walk takes you past some of the most interesting cultural attractions, providing a varied introduction to the sights of San José.

Allow 1 hour walking time, but at least half a day to explore all the attractions. See map on p28 for route.

Start at Parque Central.

1 Parque Central, Catedral Metropolitana, Teatro Mélico Salazar

Tiny Central Park (*see p35*) is more a meeting point than a park. From here you will see the cathedral, a minimalist whitewashed building with a columned

The neoclassical cathedral

façade, on the east side and Mélico Salazar theatre (*see p34*), a sunny yellow neoclassical-style building to the north. *Facing the theatre, turn right on Avenida 2. Soon the Plaza de la Cultura is on your left.*

2 Plaza de la Cultura and Teatro Nacional

The Culture Plaza is not very attractive, but as the roof of the Gold Museum and the site of the famous National Theatre (*see p34*) it seems aptly named. The theatre is an architectural attraction as well as the most important performance space in the country. *Turn left onto Avenida 2, walk around the outside of the plaza. The Museo de Oro Precolombino is down some steps on Avenida Central.*

3 Museo de Oro Precolombino

This museum (*see p31*) is a hidden treasure tucked away inconspicuously underneath the Plaza de la Cultura in a cellar-like building.

Walk back up the steps, turn left then right into the pedestrianised area of Avenida Central. The Mercado Artesanal is ten minutes' walk on your right.

4 Mercado Artesanal

This small arts-and-crafts market (*open: daily 9am–6pm*) is a good place to pick up bargain souvenirs.

At the end of the market, turn left back onto Avenida 2, walk past the concrete space of Parque de la Democracia. Across the road is Nuestra Tierra (see p160), a welcoming choice for a traditional Costa Rican lunch.

5 Museo Nacional de Costa Rica

Before turning left onto Calle 17 for the entrance to the National Museum (*see p30*), look at the outside of the building the museum is housed in, the Bellavista Fortress. The dents in the north side are bullet marks from an army mutiny in 1931 and the civil war of 1948.

Turn left out of the museum, walk north, crossing Avenidas Central and 1. Parque Nacional is in front of you.

6 Parque Nacional

This peaceful green park (*see p36*), shaded by tall trees, makes for a restful break. In the centre of the park is the Monumento Nacional, relating to the battles of 1856–7.

Turn left onto Avenida 3 at the northwest corner of the park. The Museo de Arte y Diseño Contemporáneo is on your right.

A sculpture at the Bellavista Fortress

7 Museo de Arte y Diseño Contemporáneo

The Contemporary Art and Design Museum (*see p29*), which mainly showcases the work of modern artists from across Central America, is another example of a cultural attraction incorporated into an historic building. Here the building is the old National Liquor Factory, built in 1887.

Exit the museum, turn right and walk for a few minutes to Parque España. Turn right, cross the park then Avenida 7 to reach the Jade Museum.

8 Museo del Jade

The Jade Museum (*see p30*) is famous for displaying the largest collection of American jade in the world. The pieces are exquisite, and accompanying plaques provide educational information about indigenous history.

Walk: The cultural centre, San José

Theatres

San José is the performance centre of Costa Rica and the vast majority of the country's theatres are scattered around the capital. Ticket prices tend to be comparatively cheap and there is a wide variety of plays, dance and musical performances to choose from. Apart from the National, most theatres are small and all performances are in Spanish except for those by the Little Theatre Group (*tel: (506) 289 3910*). Check the *Tico Times* for listings in English of theatre and other entertainments. *La Nación* on Thursdays and the free *Guía de Ciudad* also list events.

The Teatro Nacional in the Culture Plaza

Teatro Mélico Salazar

Dating from the 1920s and named after a coffee baron, this theatre is one of the most popular in the country. It hosts plays, classical music concerts, modern and classical dance productions and folk shows (*see p145*). *Av 2, Calle Central 2. Tel: (506) 233 5434. www.teatromelicosalazar.go.cr*

Teatro Nacional

The construction of the National Theatre is a story of wounded national pride, inspired in 1890 by a slight from the famous starlet Adelina Patti, who skipped Costa Rica in her tour of the Americas because the country had no appropriate theatre. Within a few years the rich coffee elite, by the means of export tax, had raised the necessary funds to call in European architects, engineers and artisans to design their grand vision. Today, the building remains impressive, inside and out, a monument of unrestrained elegance. Neoclassical stone columns, imposing marble staircases, plush red carpets and lavish gold detailing all add to the effect. The ceiling of the main lobby is covered in a mural fancifully depicting coffee and banana harvests, a reminder that you are in Costa Rica and not Europe. Visitors are welcome to wander around the building, although the admission costs almost as much as some of the performances. The theatre stages dance, opera, music by the National Symphony Orchestra, Latin American music and other cultural events as well as plays. *Av 2, Calle 3–5. Tel: (506) 221 5013. www.teatronacional.go.cr. Admission charge.*

THE NATIONAL FLAG

The national flag was designed in 1848 by the wife of the then president, who drew her inspiration from the French national flag and the ideals it represents. Costa Rica's flag has five symbolic horizontal stripes: blue, white, red, white and blue. The red stripe in the middle is twice the width of each of the others and represents both the warmth of Costa Ricans and the blood shed before freedom was achieved. The white stripes stand for the peace of the country and other attributes including wisdom and happiness, while the blue symbolises the sky, eternity, spirituality and qualities such as perseverance.

Parks and monuments

Although San José does not immediately impress as a green city, there is actually a series of small parks and paved plazas in the centre to provide a welcome respite from the traffic. In addition, there are several pleasant larger parks located a little further out.

Parque Central and Catedral Metropolitana

At the centre of the palm tree-dotted square that is Central Park stands a bizarre bandstand-style sculpture, donated by a former Nicaraguan dictator. Overlooking the square from the Calle Central is a completely different type of structure, the imposing white Metropolitan Cathedral. This photogenic building is fairly modern, although designed in a classical style, combining influences of neoclassical, Greek Orthodox and baroque architecture.

Parque Metropolitano La Sábana

La Sábana is a renovation success story. Once the site of San José's airport, it is now a peaceful green retreat for Josefinos and tourists who want to escape the bustle of the city without leaving it altogether. The park is dotted with tropical eucalyptus trees, characterised by the jigsaw of pastel colours in their bark. A lagoon and fountain add to the scenery, making La Sábana an attractive spot for a picnic or a stroll. There is often a football game in progress and a selection of sports facilities is also available. It is not advisable to come here at night, however, as mugging is a risk.

The sculpture in Parque Central

San José

Parque Nacional

This small but pretty national park is an oasis of cobbled paths and fountains conveniently situated near several of the city's museums. It benefits from a slightly raised elevation and the shade of conifer trees, keeping the traffic fumes at bay. In the centre of the park is a monument to the 1857 victory of the Central American nations over William Walker.

Markets

San José has an array of markets, selling everything from fruit to craft items and souvenirs. Visiting a market is a good way to get a taste of Latin American culture and pick up bargains, although the same basic issue applies as in most narrow, crowded areas, namely an abundance of pickpockets. The market culture also spills out of the halls, with street vendors selling their wares on pavements throughout the city.

Mercado Central

The biggest market in San José is the place to go to experience an assault on the senses. There is a constant stream of people wandering down the narrow aisles, although certain times of day are more chaotic than others (lunchtime in particular). The fruit and vegetable stalls are the most colourful, piled high with a vast choice of tropical produce. Stop for a cheap breakfast or lunch at one of the counters and watch the world go by.

Districts and suburbs

Barrio Amón

The business district of Barrio Amón is one of the safest and calmest places to stay in the city. It has the advantage

The lagoon at La Sábana

View of San José from Escazú

of being within walking distance from the centre, but it is significantly quieter and less chaotic. There are various hotels and restaurants around, many of which are converted from the old colonial mansions that characterise the district.

Centro Comercial El Pueblo

Located to the northeast of the city centre, near Barrio Amón, El Pueblo is a colonial-style shopping and nightlife complex. It is popular with both visitors and locals for a spot of shopping (mainly for craft items and souvenirs), eating and drinking. Next to El Pueblo is the Spirogyra Jardín de Mariposas (butterfly garden; *open: 8am–4pm, admission charge*).

Escazú

The hillside suburban town of Escazú is one of the wealthiest places in Costa Rica, popular with both rich Ticos and expats from the USA. The area is largely residential, but there is a choice of mid-range to top-end hotels, which have the advantageous combination of proximity to the city centre with panoramic views. Despite its modern aspect, Escazú is steeped in superstition and folklore. One of the local legends holds that a demon monkey called Mico Malo will haunt quarrelling couples until they resolve their differences, while another says that lonely men are at risk of being pursued by a witch named Zegua who was jilted when mortal and now seeks revenge.

San Pedro

San Pedro is the university district, and travellers comfortable socialising with students might like to sample the bars and clubs. Even if this is not your thing, the district has many conveniences, including shopping centres, cinemas and internet cafés. It is also widely considered to boast some of the best restaurants in the city.

Central Valley and Highlands

'Best climate in the world'

United Nations survey describing village of Atenas

Travelling through the pretty countryside of the Central Valley and sloping highland peaks, it is hard to believe that you are in a tropical country. The rolling green fields would not look out of place in many areas of Europe and the houses at the higher altitudes resemble alpine chalets.

Yet if any region can be said to characterise everyday life in Costa Rica, it is this one. Approximately two-thirds of the country's population live in the relatively tiny area of the valley, enclosed by mountains in a temperate microclimate that is ideal for agriculture. Outside of the urban centres of San José, Alajuela, Heredia and Cartago, rural life is centred on the production of an intriguing variety of crops. Most famous are the sweeping coffee plantations, seas of green dotted with red cherries, tied in as they are to

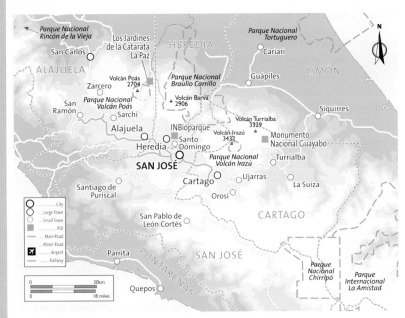

The rolling hills are reminiscent of Europe

Costa Rica's history and economy. Fields of strawberries, ferns, flowers and dairy farms all thrive at different altitudes, and a short drive up the winding mountain roads is like a whistle-stop tour through entirely diverse regions.

Many of the high peaks that dominate the landscape are sprawling volcanoes, and it is possible to drive to the summits of two of these, Irazú and Poás, both of which are active and bubbling away. The last major eruption in this area was from Irazú in 1963, but Poás occasionally blows ash high into the air. In recent years modern industries, including a large microchip production factory, have begun to spring up around the region and tourism is also beginning to take root. However, Costa Rica's heartland retains its charm and visitors are rewarded by an experience of cultural authenticity as well as unique scenery and idyllic weather.

Alajuela

Costa Rica's second-largest city is only about 18km (11 miles) from San José, but has its own individual character. Alajuela is famed primarily as the birthplace of the national hero, who is commemorated by the small Museo Juan Santamaría and with a statue in

Statue of Juan Santamaría in Alajuela

JUAN SANTAMARÍA

In 1856 an American called William Walker, who was attempting to privately colonise the whole of Central America, led his troops into Costa Rica. Among the civilians mobilised to fight against him was young Juan Santamaría from Alajuela, who joined the volunteer army as a drummer boy. Santamaría was killed while setting fire to a building which Walker's troops were using as their stronghold, helping to drive the invaders out of the country. Almost 50 years later the victory had become legendary and Santamaría was named as the national hero of Costa Rica. His bravery is commemorated with a national holiday on 11 April, the anniversary of his death.

Cartago

Costa Rica's colonial capital, founded in 1563, was reduced to a shadow of its former architectural glory by the eruption of Irazú in 1723 and two subsequent earthquakes in 1841 and 1910. Cartago's river valley setting is still beautiful, but there is not much to interest visitors in the city itself. The only truly noteworthy building is the Basilica de Nuestra Señora de Los Angeles, which holds great religious significance as the home of the dark stone statue, La Negrita. The story goes that the statue was found by a young woman on 2 August 1635 and that each time she tried to take it home, it reappeared at the place where she found it. The people of Cartago, seeing this as a sign, built the basilica on that same spot, and some time later the statue was made the patron saint of Costa Rica. Every year on 2 August pilgrims shuffle the 22km (14 miles)

the Parque Juan Santamaría. Due to a mix-up when the statue was made, it is not actually a representation of how Santamaría looked, but it's the thought that counts! Known as the city of mangoes because of the proliferation of mango trees in its centre, Alajuela retains a strong link to the agricultural traditions of the region while simultaneously functioning as a modern city. The 19th-century buildings around the Parque Central are worth a look. Alajuela is vulnerable to earthquakes, so buildings are kept to a maximum of two storeys.

Museo Juan Santamaría *Av 3, Calle 2. Tel: (506) 441 4775. Open: 10am–6pm Tue–Sun. Free admission.*

from San José to Cartago on their knees to worship it, and devotees also believe that it has the power to heal.

The city is also home to Universidad Nacional (the National University) and has a large student population.

Heredia

Heredia is close to San José in distance but distinctive in style. Founded in 1706, the colonial Ciudad de las Flores (City of Flowers) flourished in line with the coffee industry. In recent years, microchips have joined coffee as Heredia has grown increasingly high-tech, but it remains one of the prettier cities in the country. Typically, the main attractions are the old buildings situated around the Parque Central. Among these is Heredia's official symbol, El Fortín, a 140-year-old guard tower with curious peepholes that face the wrong way, once part of a fortress but never actually put to use in a battle.

INBioparque

INBio is Costa Rica's National Biodiversity Institute, a non-profit organisation dedicated to scientific research and promoting the importance of conserving the country's rich biological diversity. INBioparque was set up as an educational resource for tourists and locals. The park is not intended as a substitute for exploring wild habitats; instead it serves as a useful introduction. It is particularly popular with families, groups of schoolchildren and students, although adults are likely to find that they too have much to learn from the knowledgeable guides. Tours start

A red frog at INBioparque

with a short video presentation about INBio and biodiversity in Costa Rica, before leading visitors along a series of trails through different types of tropical forest and past a lagoon. Residents include poison dart frogs, butterflies, iguanas, snakes and ants. There is also a small working farm, with animals, intriguing medicinal plants and a sugar-cane mill. Well-equipped facilities include a canteen, café and shop.

Santo Domingo de Heredia. *Tel: (506) 507 8107. www.inbioparque.com. Open: Tue–Sun 8am–6pm (last admission 4pm). Admission charge (child/student discount).*

Los Jardines de la Catarata La Paz

La Paz (meaning peace) Waterfall Gardens is located on the eastern slope of Poás volcano and makes another extremely popular day trip. The gardens are based around a cascade of five stunning waterfalls as Río La Paz makes a rapid 1,400m (4,593ft) descent. Manageable trails and steps lead visitors down to the waterfalls via an assortment of other attractions, and a shuttle bus then brings you back up to the visitor centre at the entrance. Hummingbird and orchid gardens are among the non-watery diversions, as well as a fascinating butterfly conservatory,

The tranquil Jardines de la Catarata La Paz

A hummingbird at the waterfall gardens

frog and snake houses and countless flowers. Filling and varied lunches are available at a decent canteen.
Tel: (506) 265 0643.
www.waterfallgardens.com.
Open: 8.30am–5.30pm. Admission charge (child/student discount).

Monumento Nacional Guayabo

Guayabo National Monument is the most significant archaeological site in Costa Rica. It was discovered at the end of the 19th century, but excavations did not begin until the late 1960s and are still continuing today, with much of the site remaining unexplored due to lack of funds. Mystery surrounds Guayabo and it is not known which group built it or why it was subsequently abandoned, although it is thought to have been occupied from 1000 BC to

AD 1400. So far, the unearthed ruins include an impressive aqueduct system, pottery and petroglyphs carved on stones. Gold objects have also been found and are now on display at the National Museum.
Tel: (506) 559 1220. Open: 8am–3.30pm. Admission charge.

Parque Nacional Braulio Carrillo

Braulio Carrillo National Park was established in 1978 to protect a rugged expanse of dense mountainous forest. This vast area of 85 per cent primary forest was at risk from a proposed new highway to link the capital to Puerto Limón. Fortunately a compromise was reached; one road was built but the national park was created to prevent any further development. Despite the park's proximity to San

Flora

Costa Rica is host to an amazing variety of flora – it has as many identified species as there are in the whole of Europe. It is currently estimated that there are over 10,000 species of plants and trees in the country, a number of which are globally endangered, and the figure is constantly growing as more species are discovered.

The most endangered of the country's ecosystems is the tropical dry forest of the northwest, a unique woodland habitat that has been made rare by widespread deforestation. In the surviving forests of Guanacaste one of the most spectacular sights is created by the flowering trees, which bloom sporadically between November and May forming clouds of white, pink, yellow, purple or red in the midst of the dry landscape. The tropical dry forest also contains ancient tree ferns, a species that has been around since dinosaurs walked the Earth.

The humid forests found in other parts of Costa Rica are fascinating places, characterised by their sheer greenness, with plants growing layer upon layer. A huge percentage of the plant life in rainforests is in the lofty

Dwarf cloud forest at the Laguna Botos

Costa Rica's national flower, *guaria morada*

canopy, but this is hard to believe when walking through the dense green tangle of leaves, vines and roots at ground level. Some of the roots – those attached to walking palm trees – even move across the forest floor.

Vegetation in the cloud forest is even more layered, as it has adapted to the fact that there is more moisture in the air than in the ground. Epiphytic mosses, ferns and flowering plants often completely shroud the tree trunks from view. Epiphytes (plants which grow on other plants) are a weird and wonderful phenomenon found in some plant families, especially bromeliads and orchids. Bromeliads have broad spiky leaves (the pineapple is an example), often in vibrant colours, and hold a reservoir of water which acts as a

drinking well for animals. One of the most intriguing trees is the hollow strangler fig tree, which thrives by growing around and then killing a 'host' tree. Besides the cloud forest a good place to see these is Rincón de la Vieja Park (*see p71*).

Orchids account for over 1,200 of the country's floral species. The national flower is the *guaria morada*, a purple orchid, while other interesting varieties include 'dracula', so called because of its long, dark-red petals, and 'dutch man's shoe', which resembles a clog. Many orchids are literally microscopic and the cloud forest is a good place to see these fascinating miniature flowers.

Throughout Costa Rica a good variety of vibrant tropical flowers can be seen, including pretty hibiscus, exotic passion flowers, bright-red ginger flowers and distinctive heliconias. Another common plant is the 'poor man's umbrella' (*sombrilla de pobre*), which, as the name suggests, has massive leaves. Wild avocado, almond and coconut trees are among the wealth of natural food sources for animals and people.

Some of the most extraordinary plants are found in coastal swamp areas and include five species of mangrove trees as well as floating plants such as the water hyacinths found in Tortuguero National Park (*see p98*).

José, the sweeping mountain forest, deep canyons and plunging waterfalls of Braulio Carrillo are not much visited. However, a drive along the scenic road through the park gives an insight into what Costa Rica used to look like just 60 or so years ago when three-quarters of the country was covered in forest. There is a choice of ranger stations (*puestos de guardías*) on the outskirts, from where you can follow trails of varying lengths and difficulties into the park. The Braulio Carillo area includes dormant Volcán Barva, which is less accessible than some of the other volcanoes in the Central Highlands. A signposted trail leads from the Barva entrance up to the three lagoons of the summit, a fairly steep and often muddy climb of about an hour. The area is also home to the 2.6km (1½-mile) Rainforest Aerial Tram, a pricey but fun (and surprisingly environmentally considerate) venture that takes riders up into the forest canopy.

Ranger stations open 7am–4pm. Admission charge. Zurquí Tel: (506) 257 0992. Quebrada González Tel: (506) 233 4533. Barva Sector Tel: (506) 261 2619. Rainforest Aerial Tram. Tel: (506) 257 5961. Admission charge (student/child discount).

Parque Nacional Volcán Irazú

At 3,432m (11,260ft), Irazú is the tallest active volcano in Costa Rica and it has a long history of causing destruction, particularly with the eruption that devastated the city of Cartago in 1723. It has been simmering away more or less quietly since its last major eruption in 1963, when the Central Valley was covered in a thick duvet of ash. The craters are the only real attraction in the park, and the best time to see them unconcealed by cloud tends to be early in the morning. Facilities are limited to an information centre and a café, so Irazú is not really a whole-day activity.

Tel: (506) 551 9398. Open: 8am–3.30pm. Admission charge.

Parque Nacional Volcán Poás

Poás, one of the most easily reached active volcanoes in the world, is the key feature of the most popular national park in Costa Rica. On a clear day the view at the summit is breathtaking, although it is difficult to grasp the sheer size of the crater, which is 1.3km (¾ mile) across with a depth of 300m (984ft). This sulphuric lunar landscape is far from static; it was shaped as recently as 1953, when the volcano last erupted, and the colour of the water in the cauldron is subject to mineral changes. The summit is 2,704m (8,871ft) above sea level so temperatures range from mild to cold. Early morning tends to be a good time to beat the clouds that often obscure the view, but a perfect view cannot be guaranteed. However, the weather can change rapidly and clouds roll out as well as in.

Poás also has two other craters, although these are no longer active. The Sendero Botos trail leads from the main summit through quirky dwarf cloud forest to the icy blue Laguna Botos, which fills one of the old craters. There is one other main trail, Sendero Escalonia, which is longer and less popular.

Open: 8am–3.30pm. Admission charge.

Volcán Poás's huge crater

Tour: San José to Volcán Poás

Driving to Poás you will get a sense of the scenic, cultural and agricultural landscape of the Central Valley and Highlands, as well as enjoying panoramic views as the route winds towards the volcano's summit. You can do the tour independently or with a guide.

Aim to get to Poás before 10am. Allow two hours for the drive plus brief stops. Allow 30 minutes for the round-trip walk at the summit.

Start in San José. Take the Interamericana road towards Juan Santamaría International Airport. The turn-off for Alajuela is on the right before the airport.

1 Juan Santamaría statue, Alajuela

The statue is located in Parque Juan Santamaría, which is on the east side of Calle 2 between Avenidas 2 and 4, and can be seen from the road.
Drive straight ahead along Calle 2 for two blocks to get to Parque Central (on the right).

2 Parque Central, Alajuela

Take in the pleasant atmosphere of breezy Alajuela in the tree-encircled Central Park. Several of the surrounding buildings date from the 19th century, including the earthquake-damaged cathedral to the east. Opposite the northern edge of the park is Museo Juan Santamaría, housed in a whitewashed former prison building. The museum does not open until 10am.

From Alajuela take route 130 about 6km (3¹/₂ miles) north towards San Isidro, following the road towards Dulce Nombre. After 2km (1¹/₄ miles) the road sweeps round to the left. The shop and café for the Doka Estate are after the bend.

3 Doka Estate

The Doka Estate produces the award-winning *Café Tres Generaciones* (Three Generations Coffee), so called because it is a family-run business dating back 60 years or so. The shop overlooks the plantation – a gorgeous vista. You can reserve a place on a tour, or simply admire the view before choosing from the array of different coffee blends on sale.
Tel: (506) 449 5152.
www.dokaestate.com. Tours throughout

the day (9am–3.30pm). Phone or email to book and for directions.
Continue on the road for about 4km (2½ miles) until it forks. Take the right fork to join the main road to Poás, just before Fraijanes.

4 Fraijanes route

The pretty town of Fraijanes is famous locally for strawberry milkshake. Along the road to Parque Nacional Volcán Poás there are usually roadside stalls selling fresh strawberries, as well as assorted

other picnic temptations. This is a very scenic mountain route and provides a taste of Costa Rican country life.
Turn left for Poás (see p46) soon after passing Fraijanes.

5 Volcán Poás

A short walk from the car park and visitor centre is a lookout point over the rocky active crater of Poás volcano, an awe-inspiring sight.
Walk a short way back down the access path. Turn left onto Sendero Botos. Follow the trail (about 15 minutes) to a lookout point over the lake.

6 Laguna Botos

Contrasting dramatically with the active crater, the old Botos crater is a bowl of lush green vegetation with a sparkling blue lake as the centrepiece.
La Paz Waterfall Gardens (see p42) is a good attraction to combine with Poás. Outside the park, turn left towards Poasito, left again towards Varablanca and straight up the road to La Paz. Alternatively, consider driving directly to Poás in the morning, making the suggested stops on your return trip.

Los Jardines de la Catarata La Paz

Parque Nacional Braulio Carrillo

Cinchona

Río Sarapiquí

Parque Nacional Volcán Poás

Volcán Poás 2704

Laguna Botos

Cerro Cacho Negro 2150

Varablanca

Poasito

Volcán Barva 2906

Fraijanes

ALAJUELA

Dulce Nombre

Doka Estate
San Isidro

Carrizal

130

HEREDIA

Alajuela

Santa Bárbara

Heredia

Juan Santamaría

San Vicente de Moravia

Pozos

SAN JOSÉ

San Pedro

Hatillo

SAN JOSÉ

Desamparados

City
Large Town
Small Town
Start of Tour
Tour
Main Road
Minor Road
Airport
Railway

0 .... 12km
0 .... 6 miles

The story of Costa Rican coffee

Since the 19th century Costa Rican coffee has been exported around the world and is widely famed for its quality. This popular drink has had a huge impact on the country's history and development. Costa Rica was largely overlooked by the Spaniards, who considered it one of the least profitable outposts of their empire, but the country's fortunes began to change dramatically at the beginning of the 19th century. The discovery that the fertile volcanic soil and fresh climate of much of inland Costa Rica, primarily the Central Valley, provided the perfect environment for the cultivation of coffee beans was a momentous one. By the time of independence in 1821 the first beans had been exported and the government, realising the potential of developing a full-scale coffee industry, was strongly promoting the idea by handing out free saplings to farmers in the Central Valley. Throughout the 1830s the beans were sent to South America to be processed and mixed with other varieties before being transported on to Europe, but in 1844 local growers seized their chance to send a visiting English merchant back to London with a large cargo of coffee. It was an instant hit and word soon spread internationally; a trade had begun that would see once impoverished Costa Rica transformed into the wealthiest nation in Central America by the end of the century.

Coffee barons prospered by taking control of the trade elements, but the benefits of the industry's success were also reaped to a lesser extent by the small-scale growers. In this respect the country differed from the rest of Central America, where small elite

Coffee beans are distinctive for their red colour

Coffee plantations dominate the landscape in the Central Valley

groups monopolised every aspect of production and labourers remained poor. Apart from greatly boosting the economy, the coffee industry also directly influenced politics, infrastructure and culture. The colourful painted ox-carts that were made in Sarchí to transport coffee to Puntarenas dock became a national symbol and are still in use today, as well as being showcased at an annual festival and imitated in miniature for souvenirs (see p146). In the 1890s, some time after the heyday of the ox-carts, the wealthy coffee barons, who dominated national politics, established an export tax to finance the creation of another cultural icon, the Teatro Nacional in San José.

At around the same time the San José–Puerto Limón railway opened and trains began to transport coffee to the Caribbean port for an easier export route across the Atlantic. The railway was constructed by a workforce of mainly Jamaican immigrants and it is therefore due to coffee that Limón province is such a multicultural place. Today, after filtering through the country's history and culture for two centuries, coffee remains highly significant and the industry continues to evolve. In 1988 COOCAFE (Consortium of Coffee Cooperatives of Guanacaste & Montes de Oro) was founded as a coalition of nine producer co-operatives selling to the Fair Trade market. As they receive a fair price for their coffee, these small co-ops (who, despite Costa Rica's relatively positive model, are still disadvantaged against bigger market players) are able to grow and to support educational and environmental projects in their communities.

Painted ox-carts are one of Sarchí's specialities

Sarchí

Sarchí is the crafts centre of the Central Valley, famous as the home of the traditional painted ox-cart. Today the souvenir industry is in full swing and the carts are made in large *fábricas de carretas* (ox-cart factories) while furniture, another Sarchí staple, is crafted in *mueberías* (furniture factories). Although Sarchí village is more industrial than quaint, there is a pretty pastel church perched on the hill at Sarchí Norte. A smattering of workshops in the surrounding countryside presents a different angle to the crafts trade for those who venture a little further out.

Turrialba

Turrialba is a calm mountain town where coffee is still bigger business than tourism. However, the town is located close to some significant attractions, principally Guayabo monument and two rivers with excellent whitewater rafting, Reventazón and Parcuaré. Dormant Volcán Turrialba is not very accessible, but it does cut a striking silhouette, and most of the hotels in the area arrange guided horse rides or hikes up it.

Valle Orosí

The lovely Orosí valley, surrounded by hills and waterfalls, offers a great opportunity for a picturesque drive if you are in the area. Good stopping points include the hot spring swimming pools of Orosí village and the ruined church at Ujarrás.

Zarcero

The main attraction in the refreshing high-altitude town of Zarcero is the unique topiary garden at Parque Francisco Alvarado. After spending some time wandering around the eclectic collection of sculpted foliage and admiring the crisp mountain scenery, you will probably have worked up an appetite for the organic strawberries and cheese for which Zarcero is also known.

HAUNTING LEGENDS

Many Costa Rican legends are cautionary tales, traditionally told to prevent young people straying from the moral path. Once upon a time a youth in Cartago was cursed by his father because of his wild partying and turned into a giant black dog with red eyes known as El Cadejos, which haunts those drinking excessively. La Segua is a phantom of a beautiful woman who was jilted and exacts revenge on lone men at night by turning into a monster after they offer her a ride. The sad legends of La Llorona, who haunts rivers after throwing her baby in one, and Tulevieja, who looks for babies to feed after neglecting her own, warn against young girls getting pregnant.

Organic strawberries on sale in Zarcero

Central Valley and Highlands

Central Pacific and southern Nicoya

The central Pacific coast has long been a popular holiday destination with both Ticos and visitors, and it is one of the busiest parts of the country. Surfers and sport-fishers are drawn to the wild attractions of the ocean, while families and sunbathers enjoy the white-sand beaches. It is important to be aware, however, that the central Pacific region experiences some of the worst riptides in the country and many of these beautiful beaches do not offer safe swimming. Always check local advice and obey signs that warn against going in the sea.

This small region is decidedly tropical, with sultry temperatures practically year-round and downpours in the wet season. Although the scenery is not as spectacular as in other parts of Costa

Rica, its beauty is evident as Pacific waves foam at the shoreline of shimmering sandy beaches backed by lush forest. This is a transitory landscape, from the rainforest of the

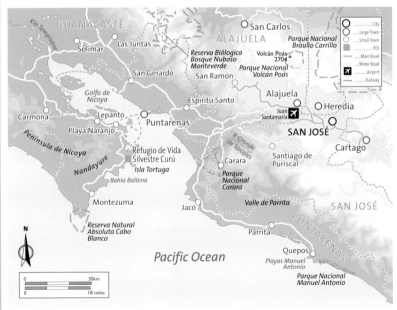

The Central Pacific coast offers lush vegetation and sandy beaches

south to the tropical dry forest common to the Guanacaste province which borders it to the north. A ferry trip across the Gulf of Nicoya takes you past the picturesque little islands clustered around the southern tip of the peninsula. The southern Nicoya peninsula boasts similarly lovely beaches to the central Pacific, but here deforestation has sadly taken hold and the coast is largely lined with agricultural land instead of trees. National parks and reserves are distributed along both coastlines, protecting a wealth of wildlife including monkeys, birds and marine creatures to tempt you away from the beaches during your stay. Tourism is an important source of income in this region, but overdevelopment is becoming a threat to the idyllic setting.

Beaches of the southern Nicoya Peninsula

The southern tip of the Península de Nicoya, a region known locally as Nandayure, is actually easier to reach by ferry from Puntarenas or Jacó than by

BEACH LIFE

All the beaches in Costa Rica are public and land within 50m (164ft) of the high-tide line cannot be privately owned. Therefore, even if a beach appears to be part of a hotel development, it is technically open to all (although access can be difficult). The government has a Bandera Azul (blue flag) programme, under which beaches (and some inland communities near nature attractions) are assessed according to certain criteria such as cleanliness, security and environmental education. At the time of writing there were 56 beaches flying blue flags. A dress-code point: topless sunbathing is frowned upon, although skimpy bathing suits are fine.

driving down the peninsula. It is possible to drive across using the bridge over the Río Tempisque, but the roads are generally poor and can verge on impassable in the rainy season. Nandayure is a largely agricultural region and the least developed part of the peninsula, but there are a few popular beach towns. The beaches of Pochote and Tambor stretch around the deep curve of Bahía Ballena (Whale Bay), framed by mangroves and little fishing villages. Despite some controversial hotel developments, this is generally a peaceful area suited for relaxing breaks, swimming and sea kayaking. Whales are sometimes seen in the bay. The remote village of Montezuma first became popular as a destination for hippy-types, and a laid-back vibe still prevails.

The beaches stretching along the coast from the village in both directions are lovely, with panoramic ocean views creating a picturesque backdrop for a stroll or sunbathe, but swimming is often not safe due to riptides. There are several waterfalls south of Montezuma where it is possible to take a refreshing dip in the pools. Be cautious if swimming, and take note that it is very dangerous to climb the rocks by the falls. The village has good-value hotels, a selection of restaurants, an internet café, several small shops and tour operators. Trips on offer include diving, horse riding and visits to the Cabo Blanco Reserve or Isla Tortuga.

A spider monkey in the Parque Nacional Manuel Antonio

Isla Tortuga

Exceptionally pretty Isla Tortuga (actually two islands) is a real-life manifestation of how a tropical paradise might be imagined. Fine white sand, coconut palms, lush vegetation and warm waters ideal for swimming, snorkelling or kayaking, give the islands a wide appeal. Tortuga is uninhabited and has no accommodation, but it is a popular day-trip destination by ferry from Montezuma or Puntarenas. There are round-trip tours from San José, although these do not allow much time on the island. Weekdays tend to be quieter than weekends. Coonatramar (*Tel: (506) 661 9011. www.coonatramar.com*) arranges tours to the islands from Puntarenas.

Parque Nacional Carara

Laced with streams and swamps, the forested oasis of Carara National Park is a vital component of the Central Pacific conservation zone, as it sits at the point where the humid landscape of the south meets the dry lowlands to the north. Due to this location there is a unique combination of plants from both ecosystems in the forest. Carara hugs the southern bank of the Río Grande de Tárcoles, and one of the park's most picturesque sights is an oxbow lake covered in floating plants, the result of the river changing course. The endangered scarlet macaws are common here, along with a variety of aquatic birds. Another major attraction is the large population of crocodiles.

Many of these can frequently be spotted outside the park, sunning themselves on a sandbank beneath Río Tárcoles Bridge (or 'Crocodile Bridge').

Carara means 'crocodile' in the language of the Huetar, an indigenous group who used to live in the area. There are no longer any Huetar people here (although some survive elsewhere), but Carara park contains some small archaeological sites that they left behind. There is a lack of accommodation in the park but there is a wide choice around the nearby party and surfing beach resort of Jacó.

Entrance at Carara Ranger Station. Open: 7am–4pm daily. Admission charge.

Río Grande de Tárcoles in Parque Nacional Carara

Central Pacific and southern Nicoya

Parque Nacional Manuel Antonio

As one of Costa Rica's smallest national parks, Manuel Antonio offers a chance to experience several of the country's natural assets in a compact space. It has tropical rainforest, mangroves, hilly viewpoints, stunning beaches dotted with coconuts and an assortment of wildlife all within an area of less than 7sq km (3sq miles). It also has lots of tourists, although the numbers are limited to 600 a day on weekdays and 800 at weekends, and the park is closed every Monday for a respite. The trail near the entrance can seem crowded and Manuel Antonio rarely feels deserted, but further into the forest and on the beaches there usually seems to be space for everyone. Happily, the animals also contribute to the bustling effect; monkeys swing through branches over the walking trails and you may see a sloth clinging to a tree trunk, or a small mammal, such as a coati or peccary, shuffling through the undergrowth. One of the most important things to remember if a troop of monkeys crosses your path is not to feed them (this can cause all sorts of problems for them, from illness to aggressive and dependent behaviour) and to hold on to your belongings. The common white-faced capuchin monkeys are nature's pickpockets. On the beaches black iguanas lounge on rocks and countless crabs make an absorbing sight as they scuttle across the sand. A network of trails weaves through the park, leading down to the beaches and up to lookout points over the Pacific. The trails are not arduous, although they can be slippery, and there are many interesting plants to note along the way, from giant bamboo to bright red hibiscus flowers.

Playa Manuel Antonio in the Parque Nacional Manuel Antonio

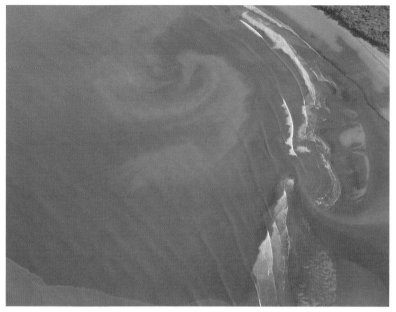

Powerful riptides are common on Costa Rica's beaches

Ranger station and information centre tel: (506) 777 0644. Open: 7am–4pm Tue–Sun. Admission charge.

Puntarenas

In its heyday in the 19th century, Puntarenas ('sandy point') was a bustling port shipping bananas and coffee. Now, fishing and tourism keep the city afloat and the waters that surround its narrow peninsula are scattered with fishing boats, cruise ships and ferries transporting travellers across to the Nicoya Peninsula. Most tourists pass through, although Tico families from the Central Valley visit. Puntarenas sizzles in the heat that characterises the central Pacific region and its buildings have a faded sun- and time-worn look. However, the city is not lacking in character, especially when festivals are taking place, and it does boast some stunning views of the Gulf of Nicoya.

RIPTIDES

Tragically, many swimmers have drowned as a result of riptides, and the prevalence of these on many of Costa Rica's beaches makes them a serious threat. The best precaution you can take is to ask locally about the safety of swimming at individual beaches. If you do get caught in a riptide, the important thing is not to panic; call for help and then float with the current until it releases you, which it will do once you are past the breakers. You should then swim back to the beach at a diagonal angle, not straight in, to avoid getting caught up again.

Walk: Parque Nacional Manuel Antonio

This walk through one of Costa Rica's smallest national parks is a great introduction to walking in the coastal rainforest.

Allow about three hours for the walk, or bring a picnic lunch and spend a day.

Start at Playa Espadilla, just outside the park, which is where buses stop.

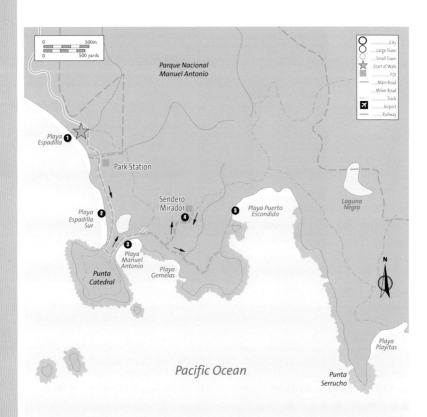

1 Playa Espadilla

Panoramic Espadilla Beach is lovely and you will see it to best advantage in the morning before the crowds descend. *There is a small river estuary to cross before the park entrance. A couple of opportunist men offer to let visitors pay to walk across their boat. Look at the stream before parting with any cash, as although it can be quite deep, at low tide it is shallow and takes just a few seconds to paddle across. After crossing the river walk to the left over a small sand hill.*

2 Playa Espadilla Sur

Playa Espadilla Sur (second beach) sweeps around the coast in a gentle arc parallel to the main trail from the entrance. This is a sandy trail, divided from the beach by coconut palms and fringed on the other side by forest. *Follow the trail to the end of the beach. Here you have an option to extend your walk by following a circular trail around the small rocky peninsula Punta Catedral. There are several little islands offshore where seabirds nest. However, this trail may be closed if weather conditions have made it too slippery. A short, well-signed path cuts across the narrow stem of Punta Catedral from Espadilla Sur to Playa Manuel Antonio.*

3 Playa Manuel Antonio

Playa Manuel Antonio (third beach) represents the best option for swimming in the park, and it is usually busy. This does not deter the black iguanas, however, which are a common sight.

At the end of Playa Manuel Antonio the trail divides. To the left is a road leading out of the park, to the right is Sendero Playa Gemelas y Puerto Escondido. Follow this trail for a short distance until it divides again, then take the left inland fork, Sendero Mirador.

4 Sendero Mirador

This trail winds uphill through the forest to a lookout point with a spectacular view of the Pacific Ocean. The trail is narrow and stepped, but for the relatively fit it is an easy climb. Look out for the vibrant red hibiscus flowers and keep your eyes and ears open for monkeys.

Retrace your steps downhill to the fork. Turn left, following the Sendero Playa Gemelas y Puerto Escondido towards the coast. For a shorter walk you could take a right turn for little Playa Gemelas, but if you continue a bit further along the trail you will reach Puerto Escondido.

5 Playa Puerto Escondido

Secluded Puerto Escondido (fourth beach) is generally the quietest of the beaches. At low tide it is a rocky horseshoe of coastline, which you can climb around, but at high tide the beach effectively shrinks to a small sandy cove. Check with the rangers about tide times if you want to walk around Puerto Escondido.

Walk back along the Sendero Playa Gemelas y Puerto Escondido to Playa Manuel Antonio and return to the entrance along Playa Espadilla Sur.

Quepos and Manuel Antonio area

Quepos town and Manuel Antonio village have undergone some major transformations over the years. Quepos has been reinvented several times from its ancient origin as the home of the indigenous Quepoa people, who were tragically wiped out by the Spanish. The town became a centre for banana-exporting, until a banana malady put an end to this by the mid-20th century. Today, palm-oil plantations have taken over from the bananas, but the thriving tourist industry centred on nearby Manuel Antonio National Park has become the main business of the area. Quepos attracts sport-fishers and it is a handy base for other travellers as well.

An iguana basks in the Parque Nacional Manuel Antonio

There are numerous hotels along the winding 7km (4-mile) stretch of road between Quepos and the park; so many that driving along the road can seem off-putting as you take in the sheer speed of development. Some efforts have been made to limit the impact of this, however, notably the installation of rope bridges across the road to enable squirrel monkeys to cross safely – achieved through the fundraising efforts of local children.

Manuel Antonio village has been transformed unapologetically into a tourist resort, with souvenir shops and stalls aplenty lining the beachfront at Playa Espadilla, just outside the entrance to the park. Although this is worlds away from the tropical paradise to be found in quieter parts of Costa Rica, there is a vibrant holiday feel to the resort of Manuel Antonio village and Playa Espadilla, if you accept it for what it is. The white-sand beach is spacious and undeniably pretty, particularly in the morning (it tends to get crowded by lunchtime), and if you want to browse jewellery and sarong stalls while sipping from a coconut then you are in the right place.

Refugio de Vida Silvestre Curú

Curú National Wildlife Refuge is a small semi-privately run oasis of vegetation located between Paquera and Tambor. It covers an area of tropical dry forest and mangrove swamps as well as sandy beaches tucked away in rugged coves. There is an abundance of birds and shore-dwelling creatures such as crabs and iguanas. A network of

hiking trails opens up opportunities of seeing mammals including monkeys and deer.
Tel: (506) 710 8236.
www.curutourism.com. Open: daily 7am–3pm. Admission charge.

Reserva Natural Absoluta Cabo Blanco

The longest-established protected area in Costa Rica, Cabo Blanco Absolute Nature Reserve is located on the far southerly tip of the peninsula about 10km (6 miles) from Montezuma. It safeguards a section of the ocean encompassing several small rocky islands, beautiful white-sand beaches and a diverse, largely evergreen, forest environment. The reserve is particularly important as a sanctuary for seabirds including pelicans, frigate birds and brown boobies. Cabo Blanco was named an 'absolute' nature reserve because originally visitors were not admitted. Visitors have now been allowed for some years, although not on Mondays and Tuesdays when the reserve is given a rest. There is a ranger hut and walking trails, but nowhere to buy food or drinks so bring these with you.
Ranger station tel: (560) 642 0093.
www.caboblancopark.com. Open: 8am–4pm Wed–Sun. Admission charge.

Playa Espadilla in Manuel Antonio village

Central Pacific and southern Nicoya

Fauna

The story behind the extraordinary diversity of wildlife in Costa Rica begins with a long-ago migration of species from both North and South America. Due to its position as a land bridge between these two vast continents, this tiny country ended up with mammals, reptiles and amphibians derived from both. The incredible variety of habitats found in Costa Rica helped in enabling so many different creatures to thrive.

The long list of resident land mammals includes five species of big cats: jaguar, spotted ocelot, jaguarondi, margay and mountain lion (or puma). The magnificent jaguar is seriously endangered, since each of these sleek predators needs a large forest territory rich in prey. Most of the country's jaguars roam the wilds of the bigger protected areas like Corcovado (*see p112*) and La Amistad (*see p111*). Jaguarondis and spotted ocelots are more numerous than jaguars, but they are shy and rarely seen. Margays and mountain lions are less reclusive, but visitors are still unlikely to encounter them.

Costa Rica's two sloth species and four monkey species are far more frequently seen, particularly in and around the national parks. The diurnal three-toed sloths and nocturnal two-

A raccoon digs in the sand

toed sloths live high up in the trees, where they spend much time sleeping. Sloths are so inactive that their fur is often covered in algae, which acts as a camouflage. The most common monkeys in Costa Rica are howlers, which are less intelligent than their cousins, but instinctive, and have the longest life spans. Howlers are often heard but not as often seen, as they live high up in the forest canopy. White-faced capuchins are the most intelligent and inquisitive of the monkeys. They are also omnivores and will happily descend to low elevations to forage among vegetation (or in the pockets of unsuspecting tourists). Sadly, capuchins have for some time been victims of the illegal pet trade, as have Central American squirrel monkeys, which are the most endangered of the four species. These notoriously cute little monkeys are now found only in a few southern forest locations, including the Corcovado and Manuel Antonio (see p58) regions. Spider monkeys, which get their name from their long limbs and ability to use their tail as a fifth limb, are also endangered, largely because of habitat loss as they can survive only in primary forest.

Other land mammals range from numerous bats to the endangered Baird's tapir (or 'mountain cow'), a

Sloths are often seen hanging from branches

distinctive, shy, heavy creature, distantly related to the rhinoceros. The forest floor, with its wealth of insects and vegetation, is home to foragers such as anteaters, armadillos, peccaries (wild pigs) and tropical raccoons.

Costa Rica's waters are also a meeting place between north and south, as the marine ecosystem here shares the biological diversity of the land and whales swim through on migratory routes from both hemispheres. Swimming with dolphins and whales was made illegal in Costa Rica in 2006 because of fears that such activities were not good for the animals, but it is often possible (although not guaranteed) to see them from boat tours. Dolphins and whales are present offshore from both coasts, but especially the southern Pacific coast. The northern Caribbean coastal area around Tortuguero National Park (see p98) is home to the endangered manatee.

Guanacaste and northern Nicoya

Guanacaste is one of the most culturally and geographically distinct regions of Costa Rica. Once part of Nicaragua, this province was joined to Costa Rica in 1824 after Guanacastecos were asked to vote for which country they would prefer to be part of. Guanacaste is believed to have had a more developed indigenous civilisation than many parts of what is now Costa Rica, but the Chorotega people who prospered in the region as well as in Nicaragua and Honduras for over 2,000 years did not survive the Spanish colonisation.

Although elements of indigenous traditions remain, the prevailing culture in Guanacaste today is that of the *sabanero* (cowboy), since cattle ranching was established in the colonial period. Dramatic deforestation has given much of this region a savannah-like appearance, covered in distinctive yellow grasses, although large pockets of tropical dry forest survive in the conservation area, which is a UNESCO World Heritage Site.

Seasonal change visibly affects the hot Guanacaste landscape, with many of the trees shedding their leaves in the drier months between December and April. The rainy season, although significantly less rainy than most of the country, is much greener and makes a refreshing time to visit. Throughout the year flowering trees sporadically sprinkle the countryside with blossom. However, it is the beaches of the northern Pacific coast which draw the most visitors, with their practically guaranteed sunshine and expanses of sand. Many of the most beautiful coastal areas have become very popular, both for short breaks and for holiday homes, and Guanacaste is developing fast. Other equally pretty beaches remain quiet, however, and some areas are protected for wildlife, most notably the endangered leatherback turtle.

Beaches

Northwestern Costa Rica is widely considered to boast some of the most beautiful beaches in the country. The winding rocky coastline of Guanacaste is lined with a choice of sandy beaches, which vary greatly in appearance and level of development. As a general rule, those on the central Nicoya Peninsula tend to be quieter and often less easily accessible than those towards the north nearer Liberia.

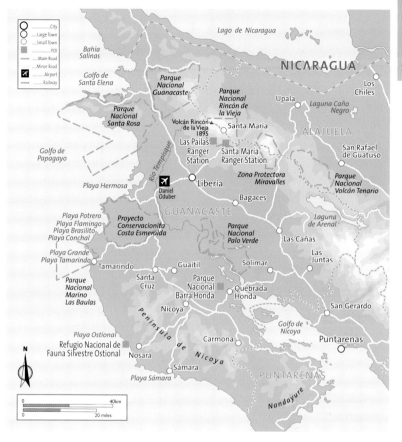

Northern beaches

Controversial tourist and real-estate developments, in the form of expensive all-inclusive resorts and timeshare villas, have marred many of the closest beaches to Liberia, such as pretty Playa Flamingo. However, there are still several peaceful, unpretentious beaches, including Hermosa, Brasilito and Playa Potrero. Playa Brasilito is not especially picturesque; instead, it offers a choice of reasonably priced hotels and a casual atmosphere, with the added bonuses of safe swimming and a short journey to prettier beaches, such as Conchal.

Playa Conchal

Often described as one of the most beautiful beaches in the country, Conchal gets its name and distinctive prettiness from the numerous shells (*conchas*) and ground-down shell fragments that blanket the sand in a layer of pastel pink. Conchal is

Sunset at Playa Flamingo

set in a sheltered bay with calm waters, which makes it an ideal spot for swimming and snorkelling. It is tricky to get to and there are not many accommodation options near the beach, but Brasilito is within walking distance (2km/1¼ miles north).

Guaitíl

The small community of Guaitíl, near the town of Santa Cruz, is the crafts capital of the region. The pre-Columbian Chorotega people made pottery here and the ancient trade was revived some time ago by a co-operative of local artisans. In keeping with the Chortega style, ceramics are made using a palette of black, cream and terracotta-red colours. You can buy them outside the potters' houses, at roadside stands or in the Artesanía

Co-operative shop. Some of the artisans also open their homes to visitors who want to watch them make the pottery.

Liberia

Liberia, the capital of Guanacaste province, still feels much like a colonial town. Many of the houses are whitewashed and one of the streets, the Calle Real (also known as Calle Central), has been partially preserved and partially restored so that it looks today more or less exactly as it did in the 19th century. Liberia was founded by farmers and cattle ranchers, and the surrounding area is still dotted with working ranches. The culture of Guanacaste is also present in many of the eateries in the town, with an assortment of shops selling traditional corn snacks and restaurants serving local food (although fast food has also arrived in Liberia en masse at the Food Mall de Burger King).

Several regional festivals are featured in the town's calendar, the liveliest of which takes place on 25 July, the day Guanacaste became part of Costa Rica, featuring horse shows, parades, *marimba* music and rodeos. Tourists generally pass through Liberia on the way to the nearby national parks and beaches, but it is also worth considering the option of staying in this safe, clean town and taking day trips around the area. Costa Rica's second international airport, Daniel Oduber, is located just outside town and operates domestic flights as well as serving as a gateway to the beaches for tourists arriving from North America.

Ostional and Nosara area

Playa Ostional is a major nesting ground for olive ridley sea turtles, and on some nights between July and November thousands of females swamp the beach to lay their eggs. The beach is protected within the Refugio Nacional de Fauna Silvestre Ostional, which extends south to the beaches around Nosara village. These scenic beaches are fringed by a verdant wildlife reserve. The whole area is fairly remote, although it does attract a reasonable number of travellers seeking a relaxing beach break.

Parque Nacional Marino Las Baulas

Las Baulas Marine National Park was established in 1991 to protect Playa Grande, a crucial and ancient nesting ground for the *baulas* (leatherback turtles), which nest here annually between November and February. These extraordinary creatures are the largest sea turtles in the world; adults can be more than 2m (6½ft) long and weigh upwards of 500kg (1,102lb). They have a life span of 50 years or more, but sadly, multiple hazards, including hunting, overdevelopment of nesting sites and plastic waste in the ocean, mean that they are gravely endangered. This national park is an uplifting example of tourism helping with

Hacienda Guachipelin, a working ranch in Guanacaste

Volcancito in Rincón de la Vieja

conservation efforts, as the entrance fees paid by visitors ensure that it remains an economically viable and hence attractive venture. Guided tours operate at night during the nesting season and can be arranged through hotels and companies in Tamarindo, as well as directly through the park. Viewing a leatherback laying and burying her eggs is a moving and memorable experience, although you will have to take a mental snapshot as photography is understandably not allowed.

Although Las Baulas is famous for its namesakes, several other types of sea turtle (olive ridley, pacific green and hawksbill) also nest at Playa Grande, while the park encompasses an area of mangrove swamp as well as the beach. The swamp includes all six different species of mangrove trees found in Costa Rica and is home to caimans,

crocodiles, howler monkeys and more than 50 species of birds.
Office tel: (506) 653 0470. Open: 9am–4pm and overnight for guided tours in nesting season. Admission charge.

Parque Nacional Palo Verde

The ancient landscape protected by Palo Verde National Park is unusual by Guanacaste standards because it is so wet. The park extends around the Tempisque river basin where the Nicoya Peninsula meets the mainland, a draining point for all the rivers in the area. A large part of the protected area is a broad grassy plain, which is often submerged by flooding in the rainy season and features a jigsaw of mangrove swamps, marshes and lakes. The dry season (December to March) is the best time to visit as this is when waterfowl and wading birds gather in huge numbers to feed and breed. Low-lying limestone hills, dating back many millions of years and cloaked in forest, overlook the plain. Palo Verde is generally more popular with birders than with tourists, but the extraordinary variety of birds here is likely to impress visitors with a casual interest as well.

Park entrance situated near Bagaces. Tel: (506) 200 0125. Admission charge. Hacienda Palo Verde Research Station (for information): Tel: (506) 661 4717. www.ots.ac.cr

Parque Nacional Rincón de la Vieja

The active Rincón de la Vieja volcano that is the centrepiece and namesake of this national park last erupted as recently as 1998, although it is not currently considered to present any danger to the area. It is possible, weather permitting, to hike up to the summit, but many interesting features of this volcanic landscape can also be experienced at base level, where the ground breathes activity. Rincón de la Vieja is one of Costa Rica's most fascinating parks, and it is not difficult, when surrounded by bubbling mud, steam and multicoloured sulphurous rocks, to imagine it as an enchanted land. Although it safeguards a rare tropical dry forest habitat, the park was created because of the wealth of water sources in the area, and the numerous streams, waterfalls and springs (both hot and cold) add to the mystical feel.

There are two main entrances to the park, at Las Pailas and Santa María ranger stations, where you can get trail

Open savannah gives way to volcanic mountains in Parque Nacional Rincón de la Vieja

Walk: Las Pailas, Rincón de la Vieja

This circular 3km (2-mile) trail will introduce you to the captivating features of Rincón de la Vieja's volcanic landscape. The walk is fairly easy going, but may not be suitable for those with mobility problems as the trail is covered in tree roots and can be slippery where it crosses streams. Set out by 2.30pm, as the park closes at 5pm.

Allow 2¹/₂ hours.

Start at the Las Pailas entrance and walk straight ahead following the trail.

1 Area de Almuerzo (picnic area)

Before the loop trail is a small picnic area with an attractive river setting by the Río Colorado. Cross the river via the little rope bridge.

Shortly after the bridge the path forks. Take the left and follow the trail through the forest. Here it becomes quite hilly. Step carefully over the tree roots as there may be columns of ants crossing

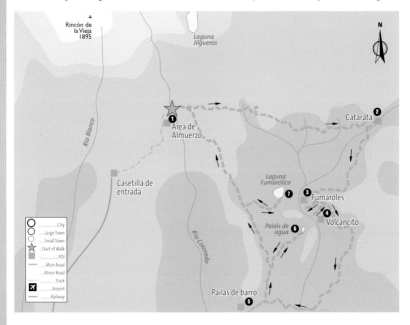

the path. Also look out for bright
orange termite mounds.

2 Catarata (waterfall)

Approximately half an hour from the
bridge the trail bends to the right by
a small but scenic waterfall, where the
Quebrada Pailas tumbles over a ridge.
You can climb up a short rocky path
to the left of the stream to get a
closer look.

Cross the stream, taking care due to
slipperiness, and continue along the
winding trail for about 15 minutes.
Turn right down a side-path signed for
the fumaroles.

3 Fumarolas (fumaroles)

The path winds alongside a fence,
with pockets of steam rising from
these openings in the ground on the
other side. At the end of the path
there is a viewing point over the
steamy fumaroles.

Walk back up the path to the main trail.
Turn right and right again onto another
short path signed to the volcancito.

4 Volcancito (little volcano)

The little volcano is an intriguing
spectacle, a pool of thick grey mud
encircled in red rock, spluttering and
exhaling steam up into the air.

Walk back up to the main trail, turn
right and continue for about 25 minutes,
going out of the dense forest cover into
a more open, savannah-like landscape.
Take the left fork signed for the pailas
de barro.

5 Pailas de barro (mud pots)

The mud pots look quite similar
to the little volcano and stimulate
several of the senses with their
sulphuric smell, bubbling noise
and the grey-and-red colour palette
of the mud.

Retrace your steps. At the fork turn
left onto the main trail. After a short
distance you will come to another
fork; turn right here for the pailas
de agua.

6 Pailas de agua (pots of water)

The *pailas de agua* are also known as
hornillas (or 'stoves'), but 'cauldrons'
would seem a more appropriate
description. These are pools of boiling
water, surrounded by colourful,
mineral-dyed, algae-coated stones.
Overhanging branches reach into
the steam, creating a scene befitting
a fantasy film.

Return to the main trail and turn
right where you rejoin it: 5–10 minutes
further on is a right turn for the
Laguna Fumarólica.

7 Laguna Fumarólica

At the end of the path you look down
on the simmering lagoon from a
viewing platform. The smell of sulphur
that permeates the area is particularly
noticeable here.

Return to the main trail and turn
right, following signs to the exit.
It is about another 10 minutes or
so to the left turn at the end of the loop
before the river.

maps. Santa María is most convenient for the popular hot springs, which are reached along the Bosque Encantado (enchanted forest) trail. The hot springs are said to have therapeutic credentials, but even so it is advisable to limit soaking time to less than half an hour and to cool off in the refreshing cold springs afterwards. Las Pailas is best for hiking to the summit or seeing the *volcancito* (mini volcano) and forest punctuated by mud pots and geysers. Take care to obey warning signs and not to step too close to any of these, as they are scalding.

Tel: (506) 661 8139. Open: 7am–5pm Tue–Sun (last admission 3pm). Admission charge.

Parques Nacionales Santa Rosa y Guanacaste

The adjacent national parks of Santa Rosa and Guanacaste protect a significant area of northwestern Costa Rica, stretching from the Península Santa Elena to the Cordillera de Guanacaste. Santa Rosa is on the coastal side and encompasses the most substantial patch of tropical dry forest remaining in Central America – savannah, evergreen oak forest and mangrove swamps. The tropical dry forest continues into Guanacaste, where it gives way to cloud forest at the higher elevations of the park. Tourists are welcome at Santa Rosa, which is rarely crowded despite its wide appeal,

A red squirrel in Santa Rosa National Park

The guanacaste is Costa Rica's national tree

but Guanacaste was set up predominantly for research and to encourage forest regeneration and has few facilities for casual visitors. For an introduction to the tropical dry forest

THE NATIONAL TREE

The province of Guanacaste was named after Costa Rica's distinctive and magnificent national tree. One of the many flowering trees of the country's driest region, the guanacaste is prized for the shade of its canopy, as well as for its attractive appearance and fragrant white blossoms. Guanacaste trees generally shed their leaves for a couple of months in the early dry season before new growth and flowers appear from late February to April. Intriguingly, it then takes nine or ten months for fruit pods to mature, and the large brown fruits are harvested from March of the following year.

habitat, try the short (1km/²/³ mile) trail, Sendero Indio Desnudo, which is near the administration centre of Santa Rosa. Various other trails lead deeper into the park, and it is worth considering hiring a guide for these as some routes are not well signed. Santa Rosa offers great opportunities for wildlife-spotting. Birds, bats and butterflies are particularly abundant, and other residents you might see include coyotes, peccaries, monkeys, raccoons and iguanas. If visiting between July and December you will have a chance of seeing olive ridley turtles nesting on Playa Nancite, although access to this amazing spectacle is restricted for the protection of the turtles, and you need to ask

The national park system

National parks, wildlife refuges and reserves account for a quarter of Costa Rican territory; an impressive statistic that has helped the country to earn international acclaim for its conservation awareness. Protected within the boundaries of these parks and reserves is an amazing range of wildlife species and habitats from cloud forests to mangroves.

The oldest protected area in the country is the Reserva Natural Absoluta Cabo Blanco, on the southern Nicoya Peninsula. Cabo Blanco Reserve was granted government protection in 1963, largely as a result of the campaigning efforts of its founders. In 1971 Santa Rosa became the first designated national park, protected as a site of historical (a seminal 19th-century battle took place here) and environmental significance.

In the mid-1990s, the national park system was organised into eight conservation areas: the Central Volcanic Mountain Range; Arenal; Guanacaste; Tempisque; Tortuguero Plains; La Amistad; Osa; and an outpost grouping of parks that did not fit neatly into the other seven areas. The Arenal area is small and dedicated to the dramatic volcanic national park of the same name, but the other conservation areas are more diverse. Within the Central Volcanic Mountain Range, besides national parks based around appealingly accessible volcanoes, there is the Guayabo National Monument,

National park entrance sign

A natural trail through Rincón de la Vieja

protected for its archaeological significance. The watery Tortuguero Plains preserves the coastal wetlands and lowland tropical forest of Tortuguero National Park, one of the oldest parks, and Barra del Colorado Wildlife Refuge. Tempisque encompasses an interesting assortment of protected areas on the Nicoya Peninsula and in southern Guanacaste, including the national parks of Palo Verde and Barra Honda. Corcovado National Park, established in 1975 to protect the last expanse of original tropical rainforest on the Pacific coast of Central America, is one of several parks covered by the Osa area.

The national parks of Guanacaste safeguard almost all the tropical dry forest that remains in Costa Rica, and the Area de Conservacíon Guanacaste, which encompasses them, has been chosen as a UNESCO World Heritage Site. Isla del Coco, the most remote of the national parks and exceptional as an Eastern Pacific island carpeted in tropical rainforest, also has this status, as does Parque Internacional La Amistad, which continues into Panama. La Amistad covers a huge and relatively unvisited area of great biological importance in mountainous southern Costa Rica.

Unfortunately, the national park system, despite all its remarkable achievements, is marred by difficulties. These fall into two main categories. Firstly there is the lack of funds, which prevents the Servicio de Parques Nacionales (SPN; National Parks Service) from comprehensively guarding all the protected areas against illegal logging and poaching. Secondly, and ironically, the tourists who provide an important source of income also put pressure on the natural environments they visit. The authorities have responded to this growing issue by setting daily limits for numbers of visitors to the most popular parks, notably the small but beautiful coastal paradise of Manuel Antonio, and individual travellers can help in a small but significant way by behaving responsibly.

Surf school in Tamarindo

permission at the administration centre. The park's scenic beaches, particularly Playa Naranjo, are frequented by serious surfers.

Santa Rosa's significance extends beyond the protection of a rare landscape; it also has a place in Costa Rican history as the site of the 1856 battle when invader William Walker was driven away, as well as two conflicts with Nicaragua in 1919 and 1955. A building called La Casona was at the centre of all this action, and although it was destroyed in a fire in 2001, it has been restored.

ACG (Area de Conservación Guanacaste) Headquarters. Tel: (506) 666 5051.
Santa Rosa: Open: 8am–4pm.
Admission charge.
Guanacaste: enquire at Santa Rosa.

Playa Sámara

Among the beaches of the central Nicoya Peninsula, Sámara is the most admired and accessible. This powdery pale sand beach is not as developed as many of the popular spots to the north, but you will find a choice of places to stay and to eat. The atmosphere at Sámara is serene, helped by the gentleness of the waves, which make it ideal for swimming and snorkelling.

Playa Tamarindo

Divided from Playa Grande by a narrow estuary, Tamarindo is one of the most popular and developed beach areas in the country, and what was once a village is now a generic tourist resort with all the usual conveniences. Consequently, Tamarindo lacks any sense of local culture, and driving into the village, past all the signs of ongoing development, can be a discouraging experience. That said, there are plenty of advantages to staying here, including sophisticated restaurants and a wide choice of ways to spend your time. Hotels and tourist companies in the area generally offer a variety of ocean-based activities as well as tours to the nearby hills, the mangrove swamp at the river estuary or Playa Grande. Most of all, Tamarindo beach itself is beautiful, particularly in the early evening as sunset stains the sky and shallow waves slide onto the shore. Despite the hordes of American (and some other) tourists who descend on it, this panoramic curve of blonde sand still has a laid-back vibe, helped by its reputation as a surf centre for beginners.

PARQUE NACIONAL BARRA HONDA

One of the country's most extraordinary national parks is Barra Honda, a vast subterranean cave network of more than 40 limestone caverns of various depths. This is a dark but fascinating environment of stalagmites, stalactites and underground creatures. The most visited cave, La Terciopelo, contains an 'organ' of stalagmites, which produces musical notes if tapped. Recently, pre-Columbian remains and burial ornaments were discovered in some of the caves, and spelaeologists have yet to fully investigate others. Tourists can visit, but only if fit enough to descend by ladder and rope, only in the mornings in the dry season and only with a registered guide.

Northern Zone

From the high-altitude cloud forest of the Monteverde protection zone to the panoramic lowland river plains extending towards the Nicaraguan border, the Northern Zone is a land of contrasts. Arguably the most powerful sight in the region, particularly on a clear night, is the classically cone-shaped and highly active Arenal volcano. Arenal and the Monteverde Reserve are major tourist magnets, regularly drawing large numbers of visitors to the north, while the wildlife-rich areas of Sarapiquí and Caño Negro also enjoy reasonable popularity.

Further afield, from the shade of the volcano throughout the plains of Guatusos and San Carlos, much of the region is focused on agriculture rather than tourism. Unsurprisingly, the Northern Zone has strong links to Nicaragua, and there are many Nicaraguan refugees working on the farms.

These links were first forged many years ago via the rivers, which have played a part in every major event

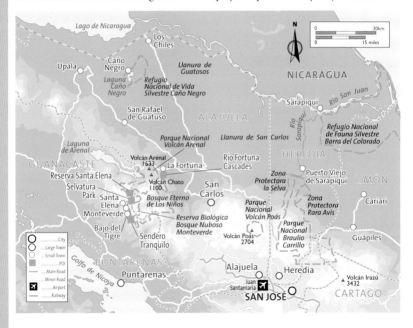

Flatland river plains near the Nicaraguan border

affecting the region. They transported the Spanish colonisers here in the early 17th century (although it would take 200 years before the Spanish really settled in the area), followed soon after by primarily British pirates, who caused turmoil. Later the rivers became a means of transport for coffee, but the region remained more tumultuous than most of the country, getting caught up in the Nicaraguan civil war. Now, the rivers weave their courses through the immense fields of pineapples, yucca, bananas, corn and sugar cane that dominate the landscape. As in Guanacaste, the effects of widespread deforestation are clear here, and forest remains only in isolated patches. However, there is a tangible charm and authenticity to this rural area where riding on horseback remains a practical form of transport and lofty sugar-cane spires frame the paths.

MONTEVERDE AND SANTA ELENA AREA

Despite the remoteness of its mountain setting, this area is one of Costa Rica's top tourist destinations. The adjoining communities of Monteverde and Santa Elena sit on a winding road, bordered by the cloud forest reserves of the same names and the vast Children's Eternal Rainforest (*see p82*). The access roads (not kind to the travel sick) have become notorious, especially since proposals to pave them were blocked by locals anxious to keep development to a manageable level. So far, this has been achieved, and, although the stretch of road that links the communities is dotted with tourist amenities, a delicate balance is being maintained.

Monteverde is home to a population of English-speaking Quakers, who arrived from the USA in the early 1950s in search of a peaceful life in this newly

Forest canopy in Monteverde Cloud Forest Reserve

army-less country. They set up a dairy farming business (producing the well-known Monteverde cheese) in harmony with the forest. Although the cloud forests are the main attraction, there is more to this delightfully quirky region than its natural wonders, namely a unique community of artists, organic farms and coffee co-operatives. Being 1,400m (4,593ft) up in the Cordillera de Tilarán means it can get chilly (generally 16–23°C/61–73°F during the day, but colder at night).

Bosque Eterno de los Niños

Measuring a vast 20,250ha (50,000 acres), the Children's Eternal Rainforest is a unique and vital conservation project funded by schoolchildren from around the world.

Since the reserve was established in 1987, the rainforest and cloud forest within its borders have been joined by new growth in areas that were cut

DISAPPEARING FROGS

In the late 1980s, a strange and alarming phenomenon happened in Monteverde and other high-altitude forest areas. A number of frogs suddenly disappeared and about 20 species are now thought to have become extinct. The highest-profile victim of the Monteverde mystery was the endemic *Sapo dorado* (golden toad), which has not been seen since 1988. It had been discovered in the cloud forest reserve only 24 years earlier. The cause of such a dramatic crash in the amphibian population has not been established for sure (although an exotic pathogen is thought the likely culprit), but one fact that has been highlighted is the fragility of the eco-balance.

down previously. As it was designed with conservation and regeneration in mind, the children's forest is almost entirely inaccessible to visitors, but there is one 3.5km (2-mile) public trail, called Sendero Bajo del Tigre (Jaguar Canyon Trail). The reserve also offers a two-hour guided twilight walk, which is a great opportunity to glimpse the glowing eyes of the unsleeping forest. The walks are popular so it is recommended to book in advance. *Tel: (506) 645 5003. Open: 7.30am–5.30pm. Guided night hike 5.30–7.30pm. Admission charge (student discount).*

Reserva Biológica Bosque Nuboso Monteverde

It is a good idea to get to Monteverde early in the morning, as there is a daily limit of 160 visitors at a time to limit stress on the delicate environment. It rains frequently in the cloud forest, and visibility through the dense vegetation is further limited by mist and cloud. This means that wildlife is elusive and it is best not to have expectations of seeing much; that way you may be pleasantly surprised. The plant life is spectacular and creates an impression that the forest is living and breathing, even if the animals stay away. The 10,530ha (26,000-acre) reserve is traversed by a network of trails of varying lengths, although most visitors stick to the short paths (up to 2km/1 mile each) that intertwine in a triangular shape near the entrance. It is easy to wander around independently,

CONTRIBUTING TO CONSERVATION

Travellers assist conservation funding by visiting the national parks and paying the entrance fees. These are not expensive and are definitely a worthwhile expenditure when you consider that the parks are maintained largely thanks to this revenue. The same is true of the entrance fee to reserves and projects like INBioparque. You can make an additional contribution with a donation to a local charitable organisation. Help protect the rainforest of the Osa Peninsula by supporting the Corcovado Foundation (*Tel: (506) 297 3013. www.corcovadofoundation.org*), which employs additional park rangers and runs other conservation initiatives. Support the Bosque Eterno de los Niños via the Monteverde Conservation League (*Tel: (506) 645 5003. www.monteverdeinfo.com/ monteverde_conservation_league*).

Northern Zone

Twenty species of frogs have now vanished from Monteverde

but taking a guided tour is beneficial as guides are knowledgeable and skilled at spotting wildlife. Reservations should be made in advance for the guided walks as they are popular.

Information office tel: (506) 645 5122. www.cct.or.cr. Open: 7am–4pm daily. Admission charge (discount children under six/students). Natural history tours: 7.30am daily. Night tours: 7.15pm daily. Birding tours: 6–11am daily from Stella's Bakery.

Reserva Santa Elena

Despite their proximity there are a few environmental differences between the Santa Elena and Monteverde reserves, due to the fact that they are actually on different sides of the Continental Divide. Santa Elena, a community-managed reserve run by the board of the local high school, is perched at a slightly higher elevation than Monteverde and is a bit wetter and warmer. Each reserve has some species which are not found in the other. Santa Elena is quieter than Monteverde and has less well-maintained, muddier trails, although these are easy enough to navigate and traverse the same ethereal landscape of densely layered vegetation. Santa Elena is supported partly through donations, and profits from the shop and café go towards conservation and environmental education for local children.

Tel: (506) 661 8290. www.monteverdeinfo.com/ reserve-santa-elena-monteverde. Open: 7am–4pm. Nature tours: 7.30am & 11.30am. Night tours: 7pm. Admission charge (student discount).

The Monteverde area hosts more than 30 kinds of hummingbirds

Treetop suspension bridge in Selvatura Park

Selvatura Park

Located near Santa Elena Reserve, Selvatura Park encompasses a sizeable chunk of primary cloud forest, which thrill-seekers can glide through on an exhilarating 15-cable zip line canopy tour. If you prefer to take your time admiring the scenery there is a circular walking trail across a series of treetop suspension bridges, which provide a different perspective on the dense forest. Selvatura has hummingbird and butterfly gardens and a reptile and amphibian exhibition house, but the prize for most captivating attraction goes to a huge insect exhibition entitled Jewels of the Rainforest. This is one of the biggest private insect collections in the world and emphasises the vibrancy and variety of some of Costa Rica's smallest inhabitants. Prices at Selvatura are not cheap, although in line with similar attractions.
Tel: (506) 645 5929. www.selvatura.com. Open: 7.30am–4pm daily. Admission charges by individual attraction.

Sendero Tranquilo

The 'Tranquil Path' private cloud forest reserve is, as the name suggests, a quiet alternative to the better-known attractions of the area. It is much smaller than Monteverde and Santa Elena, but features all the interesting plants of the cloud forest ecosystem, including chunky epiphytes, minuscule orchids and twisted strangler fig trees. Guided tours run twice a day with a maximum group size of six people and are booked through El Sapo Dorado Hotel (*see p170*). You might see hummingbirds (the Monteverde area has more than 30 species), trogons (the same family as the famous quetzal, also present but far from a guaranteed sight) and small mammals. *Tel: (506) 645 5010. www.sapodorado.com. Tours at 7.30am and 1pm. Admission charge (free for El Sapo Dorado guests).*

LA FORTUNA AND ARENAL AREA

The active Arenal volcano dominates the surrounding landscape and towns, at least when it is not shrouded in a halo of clouds. This is adventure tourism territory, with companies offering an array of outdoor activities from horse riding to abseiling down waterfall canyons and whitewater rafting. Many travellers stay in the town of La Fortuna, which, at just 6km (4 miles) away from Arenal, is truly in

The landscape around the town of La Fortuna is strikingly verdant

the volcano's shadow. La Fortuna was catapulted into the limelight after Arenal erupted in 1968, and now its main streets are lined with hotels, eateries, shops and tour operators.

Convenience is the main advantage to staying here, but it also has a pleasant atmosphere and there are other natural attractions nearby. The most picturesque of these is La Catarata de la Fortuna, where the narrow Río Fortuna cascades 70m (230ft) before splashing into a pool, framed by woodland and volcanic rock. The waterfall is about 7km (4 miles) from town and you can walk there (although it is an uphill trek), drive or take a taxi or horseback tour. A trail leads down the canyon, but the descent is steep and often slippery. Intrepid hikers will be rewarded by a stunning view, several swimming holes and a smaller waterfall, although the scene is lovely from above as well. The area around La Fortuna also boasts assorted hot springs (*see p125*). Besides the budget accommodation options in town and the generally pricier lodges around Laguna de Arenal, there are lesser-known alternatives in the village of El Castillo near the entrance to the national park, or further out in the San Carlos Plain area. *La Catarata de la Fortuna. Open: 8am–5pm. Admission charge.*

Laguna de Arenal

At 88sq km (34sq miles), Laguna de Arenal is the biggest lake in Costa Rica.

It was created in 1973 by the building of a dam to generate hydroelectricity and supply water to the parched Guanacaste province. Wind power is also supplied by the giant windmills on the hills overlooking the northern shore. The lake's creation led to several small towns being submerged and their residents relocated. The original Arenal town (redesigned at higher altitude as Nuevo Arenal) was one of the watery sacrifices, and locals say that it is possible during dry periods to see the spire of the old church rising above the surface of the lake. Laguna de Arenal contributes significant additional beauty to an already striking landscape. Fringed by cloud forest, it offers some of the best volcano views around, which, weather permitting, you can enjoy from a boat or while driving or riding along the shore (it is not possible to drive all the way around). Due to its consistent winds the lake is considered one of the top three global destinations for windsurfing, and kitesurfing is also gaining in popularity. The best months are from December to April. Equipment hire and lessons can be arranged (*see p170*).

Northern lowland plains

This little-visited area is an expanse of rivers, swamps and farmland. Furthest north is the Llanura de Guatosos, a particularly remote region bordering Nicaragua, while to the south is the Llanura de San Carlos. The rivers which lace this flat landscape provide the main attractions for travellers, with rafting and boat trips to Caño Negro being popular choices. The hub of the region is the market town of San Carlos (also known as Ciudad Quesada).

Volcán Arenal seen from La Fortuna

The volcanic landscape

Costa Rica's geographical situation at a meeting point of the Cocos and Caribbean tectonic plates signifies two dramatic things: volcanoes and earthquakes. The corridor of land that is now southern Central America first existed as a chain of volcanic islands, which gradually joined together 3–5 million years ago, linking the North and South American continents. Costa Rica is part of the Pacific Ring of Fire and has over 200 volcanoes in total, although many of these have long been extinct. The country's lush landscape was, and still is, shaped by the fiery mountains that punctuate it. A history of volcanic activity has resulted in fertile, mineral-rich soil and flourishing forests. In recent years, Costa Rica's volcanoes, particularly the active few, have become major tourist attractions. The vast majority of the volcanoes are situated in the Central Valley and in the northwestern mountain ranges.

The most active volcano in Costa Rica is Arenal, which is also considered to be in the global top ten

Arenal, surrounded by mist, seen across the Laguna de Arenal

Mud pots in Rincón de la Vieja

land that visibly exhales steam and boils just beneath the surface (*see p73*), while holes in the ground reveal cauldrons of spluttering mud.

The Central Volcanic Range is home to the only other active volcanoes in the country, Poás and Irazú. These are two of the most accessible active volcanoes in the world and it is possible to drive close to their summits. Poás and Irazú exhibit eerie but fascinating landscapes of deep craters, jagged sulphuric rock and glassy volcanic lakes. During its biggest eruption, in 1910, Poás exhaled steam, mud, rocks and ash an extraordinary 8,000m (2,625ft) up into the air. Poás had its most recent major eruption in 1953, while Irazú exploded in 1963 and continued to carpet the Central Valley in deep hot ash over a two-year period. The slopes of these volcanoes are coated in forests and farmland, a testament to the fertility of volcanic soil.

Costa Rica has a number of sleeping volcanoes, including Orosí, Tenorio, Miravelles and Barva, which show some signs of activity and could erupt in the future. Volcanoes can still cast an impressive silhouette over the surrounding landscape when they are dormant. On a clear day the sloping cone shape of Turrialba volcano can be seen looming in the distance from the Caribbean coast.

most active volcanoes. With its perfect steep conical shape and constant explosive displays, Arenal is one of the most awe-inspiring sights in the landscape. Every so often the volcano issues a reminder that it is dangerous, although the major eruption of 1968, which shook the sleeping volcano into life and devastated the local area, remains by far the biggest tragedy it has caused.

To the northwest, Rincón de la Vieja volcano steams and bubbles away. It last erupted in 1998, but unlike Arenal it is currently considered safe to get close to the summit. The area around Rincón de la Vieja, protected by the national park of the same name, is arguably the best place in the country to experience a volcanic landscape. The tropical dry forest at the base of the volcano is growing on

Tour: The Lake Trail

Despite the proximity of Arenal and Monteverde, road travel between them is long and convoluted. A number of companies bridge the gap with alternative forms of transport. As well as a speedy jeep-boat-jeep combination, there are several routes involving a horse ride for part of the way. The route below is recommended as it is safe both for inexperienced riders and for the horses, which cannot always be guaranteed with the more challenging routes.

Allow about 5½ hours for the total transfer, of which about 3 hours are spent on the horse trail.

Start in La Fortuna, where you will be picked up by a driver and taken to the shore of Laguna de Arenal to meet the boat.

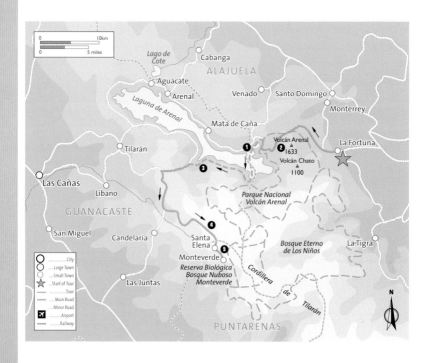

1 Laguna de Arenal

A short boat ride across the southeastern corner of lovely Laguna de Arenal makes a serene start to the trip. *On the southern shore of the lake you will be met by a guide and horses to set off on the more active part of the journey.*

2 Volcán Arenal

The southern shore of the lake provides great views of Volcán Arenal, and although your view of the summit will depend on the weather, the impressive form of the volcano looming above the water is evident in all but the thickest cloud.

3 Horse trail

This narrow winding trail hugs the shore of the lake, divided from the water by a border of vegetation. At points it feels like a woodland path, with trees rising up on either side. At other times the trees part to reveal views of the lake and volcano. The trail is mainly flat, with a few slight climbs and descents along the way. It can get muddy, so dress accordingly. There is generally a rest break about halfway through when you can get off your horse and have a snack. Just before the end of the trail you will cross a river, which is quite shallow but fast-flowing. *A driver will meet you at the end of the trail to transport you on to Monteverde by van or 4WD.*

4 Mountain route

The road to Monteverde is unpaved, mountainous and twisting, so you are in for a bumpy but beautiful drive. As the road climbs higher into the Cordillera de Tilarán you will see layers of hills and valleys stretching across Guanacaste to the west. There are a few little towns and villages along the route, but as you get closer to Monteverde it starts to feel very remote. At this high altitude the landscape is misty and densely forested. *Finally you turn a corner onto the strip of civilisation that is Santa Elena and Monteverde.*

5 Santa Elena and Monteverde

First you will pass through the village of Santa Elena, then up the winding connecting road to the community of Monteverde (depending on which hotel you are being dropped off at). The views from here are spectacular, with a combination of mountains, forests, lush fertile pastures and panoramic vistas down to the Gulfo de Nicoya.

Horse riding on the Lake Trail

Parque Nacional Volcán Arenal

In July 1968, after lying dormant for hundreds of years, Arenal volcano suddenly erupted, killing 78 people and devastating the surrounding area. Since then Arenal has stayed consistently active, emitting rumblings, ash columns and molten lava almost daily, although the level of activity varies periodically. The national park, established in 1995, encompasses a selection of trails around the volcano's base through pine forest and rainforest, where you can see the sites of old lava flows or head down to the lake. Although the landscape is the main attraction, the park is home to an abundance of wildlife. To climb to the crater would be extremely dangerous and is forbidden, but it is possible to hike to the summit at Volcán Chato, a dormant volcano just 3km (2 miles) away. The most spectacular views of Arenal are often at night when red lava glows against the dark sky, although clouds are liable to spoil the show. Tours can be arranged through various operators or you can visit the park independently via the ranger station. The Arenal Observatory Lodge, which is the only accommodation option actually inside the park, also has trails and offers guided hikes and tours.

Ranger station. Tel: (506) 461 8499. Open: 8am–4pm. Admission charge. Arenal Observatory Lodge. Tel: (506) 692 2070. www.arenalobservatorylodge.com

Refugio Nacional de Vida Silvestre Caño Negro

Caño Negro Wildlife Refuge is widely regarded as one of the best places in

Old lava flows are clearly visible on the slopes of the Arenal volcano

View over the plains of the Parque Nacional Volcán Arenal

Central America to enjoy an avian safari. The swampy landscape undergoes significant seasonal changes caused by flooding of the Río Frío. At the height of the rainy season (May–November) the land is completely submerged under a lake. January to March is the most remarkable time of year to visit, when the reserve has dried out into a marsh and extraordinary numbers of migratory birds descend to join the permanent inhabitants. Non-winged wildlife includes river turtles, iguanas, basilisk lizards, howler monkeys, bats and even big cats. Many tour operators around the region (and often further afield) offer trips to Caño Negro, or you can visit independently and ask at the ranger station about guided tours.

Ranger station at the dock.
Tel: (506) 471 1309. Open: 8am–4pm.
Admission charge.

Sarapiquí region

With the lowlands of the San Carlos plain to the north and west, humid Limón province to the east and the wilderness of Braulio Carillo to the south, Sarapiquí is a transitory region. The main town, Puerto Viejo de Sarapiquí, has little to attract travellers, but the surrounding area is interesting. Although much of the land has been deforested to make room for a vast jigsaw of fruit and *palmito* (heart of palm) plantations, a tract of primary rainforest remains within the protected reserves of La Selva and Rara Avis. These remote reserves are pristine, rich in wildlife and relatively little-visited.

Caribbean coast

Sandwiched between the Caribbean Sea and the mountainous spine of the country, Costa Rica's eastern coastal area, which forms Limón province, is different to the other coasts in several ways. In contrast to the winding Pacific shoreline with its peninsulas and islands, the Caribbean coast is smooth, joining Nicaragua to Panama in just 212km (132 miles). Yet this is one of the most biologically varied regions in the country and it has the highest proportion of protected land, encompassing jungles, mangrove swamps and coral reefs, although the huge banana and pineapple plantations do present an environmental threat. There is no real dry season to speak of along much of the Caribbean coast; it is a humid tropical zone where the distinction between land and water becomes considerably blurred.

Visitors are attracted not just to the fascinating landscape and wildlife-spotting opportunities, but also to the unique culture of the region, which is so different from that of the rest of Costa Rica that it can feel like another country. Due to an eventful history involving pirates, banana plantations, the construction of a major railway and various waves of immigrants joining the indigenous population, there is incredible ethnic diversity in Limón province. More than a third of the modern population is of Afro-Caribbean descent, and their ancestors, who came from Jamaica and Barbados in the 19th century to work on the railway, brought with them the culture and traditions of those islands. The railway that started all this was destroyed in the devastating earthquake of 1991, but its cultural legacy lives on.

Aviarios del Caribe Sloth Sanctuary

This small wildlife sanctuary is dedicated to sloths, but its coastal rainforest setting is also home to many other creatures, including monkeys and a variety of birds. Visitors can meet and learn about sloths on guided tours, and the centre also offers canoe trips along the jungle-fringed waterways of the Río Estrella delta.
10km (6 miles) north of Cahuita. Tel: (506) 750 0725. www.ogphoto.com/aviarios. Open: 6am–5pm. Charge for guided tours.

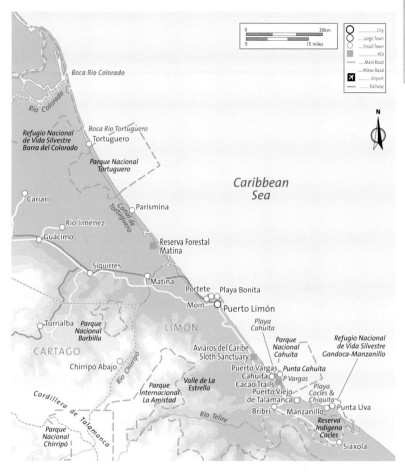

0   30km
0   15 miles

○⋯⋯City
○⋯⋯Large Town
○⋯⋯Small Town
■⋯⋯POI
⎯⎯⋯Main Road
⎯⎯⋯Minor Road
✈⋯⋯Airport
⎯⎯⋯Railway

Beaches of the southern Caribbean

The far southeastern corner of Costa Rica boasts one of the most beautiful strips of coastline in the country. The series of beaches just south of Puerto Viejo de Talamanca is known under the umbrella names of Playa Cocles and Playa Chiquita. A little further south is Punta Uva, a small hamlet with a pretty beach set in a sheltered cove. This represents one of the best opportunities for swimming in the area, as most of the beaches have wilder waves more suited to surfing. Finally there is the easy-going village and beach of Manzanillo. Accommodations and eateries fan out along the route from Puerto Viejo to Manzanillo, and the forest that spreads inland from the beaches is full of wildlife.

Cacao Trails

This fairly new attraction provides an interesting and educational excursion from Cahuita or Puerto Viejo. There is a botanical garden and outdoor museum as well as trails through cacao and banana plantations. Kayak tours are also available.

Tel: (506) 812 7460.
www.cacaotrails.com. Open: 8am–5pm.
Charge for guided tours.

Cahuita

Cahuita village is a good place to soak up the Caribbean cultural vibe as well as the sun. It makes a very convenient base for visiting the national park of the same name, which starts at the southeast corner of the village. To the north is a long black-sand beach, Playa Negra, where it is mainly safe to swim. Cahuita is popular with backpackers and has plenty of places to stay and a

Palm-fringed beach at Tortuguero village on the scenic Caribbean coast

cosmopolitan choice of restaurants. Like other spots along the coast, there is a risk of crime in Cahuita so take precautions, principally not walking alone at night or leaving valuables unattended on the beach.

Parque Nacional Cahuita

Cahuita National Park, which protects the biggest living coral reef in the country, has classically tropical beauty and a hot, humid climate to match. Just south of Cahuita village is the Kelly Creek entrance to the park, which leads on to Playa Cahuita. From here Punta Cahuita, a small spit of land, stretches out into the sea, and on the other side of this point is Playa Vargas, where the second ranger station, Puerto Vargas, is located. Both beaches consist of narrow arcs of white sand framed by a dense border of coconut palms and sea grape trees at the forest's edge. On Punta Cahuita land merges with water, creating a swampy bird haven. Howler monkeys are commonly seen (and heard) in the forest. There is one trail, following the coastline for 7km (4 miles) between the *puestos* (ranger stations), sometimes alongside the beaches and sometimes weaving deeper into the rainforest. This is generally an easy hike, but the humidity can make it uncomfortable. Be aware that the Río Perzoso crosses the trail and at high tide it can be too deep to wade across, so check with the rangers. Swimming is possible and the sea is generally quite calm, but again it is best to check.

Deserted beach near Cahuita

Sadly the coral reef is threatened, largely because of chemicals used in the inland fruit plantations, which run through the rivers into the sea, and eroded topsoil caused by logging. The 1991 earthquake also had a very harmful effect on this delicate habitat. You can visit the surviving reef on a glass-bottom boat tour or guided snorkelling trip (snorkelling is allowed only with a licensed guide). The reef is home to an array of other living things including fish, shellfish, crabs, lobsters and anemones. February through April is usually the best time of year for sea clarity.

Kelly Creek ranger station. Tel: (506) 755 0461. Open: 6am–5pm. Admission by donation (donations go towards park conservation so are important).
Puerto Vargas ranger station.
Tel: (506) 755 0302. Open: 8am–4pm. Admission charge.

Parque Nacional Tortuguero

Tortuguero (literally, 'turtle-catcher') National Park has worldwide significance as a vital nesting site for the green turtle, as well as other turtles, which led to its designation as a national park in 1975. However, there is much of interest in this wildlife-rich environment besides its most famous inhabitants. Sometimes described as a mini-Amazon, the park is built on a network of canals and lagoons, which provide the only routes through the lush tropical rainforest and mangrove swamps that stretch across the plains to the Caribbean Sea. This is one of the wettest areas in Costa Rica, a saturated tropical oasis receiving an average annual rainfall of 6,000mm (236in). There is an enchanting stillness to Tortuguero (broken only by the tour boats that traverse the waterways), and the landscape is saturated by shades of green as the tall trees of the jungle extend right to the water's edge and are reflected in its glassy surface. Monkeys and macaws are sometimes visible high up in the treetops, while aquatic birds, green iguanas and frogs thrive in the shallow, swampy vegetation at the edge of the canals. In the water there are numerous species of fish, caimans, crocodiles and critically endangered manatees.

Boat or kayak tours can be arranged through one of the nearby lodges or through tour operators in Tortuguero village. There is only one short public walking trail through the park: the well-signed but muddy El Gavilan, accessible from Cuatro Esquinas ranger station. Tortuguero beach is

Tortuguero National Park, an important habitat for the green turtle

A caiman in a Tortuguero swamp

characteristic of much of the Caribbean coast, with wild, shark-visited waters (needless to say, not safe for swimming) and sloping sand scattered with driftwood and coconuts.

Admission charge (three-day tickets available).
Cuatro Esquinas station, north of village. Tel: (506) 709 8086. Open: 5.30am–6pm (closed for breakfast and lunch breaks). Maps and information provided.
Jalova station, south entrance. Open: daily 6am–6pm.

Puerto Limón and around

The capital of Limón province is a port city with a turbulent history and neglected aspect. Long-standing isolation from the rest of the country, economic destitution in the 1930s and the devastating earthquake of 1991 all left their mark. Puerto Limón (often shortened to Limón) is frequently maligned, but while it is true that the city has problems, criticisms can be exaggerated. Limón may not be picturesque, but it is interesting, particularly during a vibrant carnival week in October (*see p21*). This is a very popular event, so making hotel reservations in advance is essential.

Although Limón does not attract many visitors at other times, travellers often pass through on the way to the southern Caribbean coast or to nearby Moín harbour, where boats leave for Tortuguero. This journey can take as little as 1½ hours or it can be a leisurely half-day activity gliding slowly up the canals. It is best to book in advance, although schedules change and the routes are sometimes blocked by thick vegetation. If you are visiting Limón, recommended precautions are: avoid arriving at night, do not carry valuables or leave them in a parked car and do not drink the tap water.

If you have only a little time to spare, one of the most interesting places to see is Parque Vargas. This is a seafront park at the southeast point of the city, featuring palm trees, tropical flowers and a colourful mural with images depicting Limón's history from pre-Columbian times to the arrival of the railway. Swimming is neither possible nor appealing anywhere in the Puerto Limón area. Between Moín and Puerto Limón two small coastal communities, Portete and Playa Bonita, offer more peaceful alternatives to staying in the city, with Caribbean views and a selection of decent hotels.

The culture of the Caribbean

Visitors to the Caribbean coast can look forward to a distinctive cultural experience, which stems from the area's history and the ethnic diversity of its people. Over the years Limón province developed very differently from the rest of the country; it was seen as a separate entity, long isolated and neglected by the central government. Although the Spanish invasion of what is now Costa Rica began in this region, it took the colonisers more than 200 years to put down real roots here, hampered as they were by the pirates who favoured this coast. Local stories tell of pirate shipwrecks (there are two sunken ships to the north of Punta Cahuita) and buried treasure guarded by pirate ghosts.

Around 1870 a decision was taken to build a railway linking San José to Puerto Limón in order to transport coffee for export. The task was arduous and many of the workers (who had been recruited from various countries besides Costa Rica) died of yellow fever. However, a large number of Afro-Caribbean labourers, mainly from Jamaica, survived to finish the task, and the first 'Jungle Train' set off in 1890. The man in charge of the railway project, an American called Minor Keith, had planted bananas to

A calypso band from the Limón region

Coconuts on the beach

help with funding, and in the new, rapidly thriving banana business owned by the United Fruit Company the railway workers found jobs and a reason to settle permanently. They brought with them their own cultural and practical traditions relating to everything from language to food and made Costa Rica's Caribbean coast their home.

Life was certainly not always easy for the settlers and their descendants. Limón's Afro-Caribbean population, like the indigenous communities throughout the country, faced marked discrimination until well into the 20th century. In the 1930s the banana plantations were hit by pestilence, and, despite major worker strikes, United Fruit moved their business to the Pacific coast. The region's fortunes plummeted, but the Afro-Caribbean workers were forced to stay as they had not been given rights to live anywhere else in the country, so they resorted to fishing, subsistence farming or cocoa cultivation. Banana production eventually resumed in Limón, under a different company, and the fruit continues to have a major impact on the society and economy of the province, as well as on the environment.

In 1949 black Costa Ricans were finally given full rights to live elsewhere in the country, but most have stayed at the Caribbean coast, where they have preserved their Jamaican-derived culture while mingling with indigenous people, Nicaraguans and others to create a truly multi-ethnic society. English is the traditional language of the Afro-Caribbean population, but many people in Limón (particularly young people) speak Spanish peppered with English phrases.

One of the delights of visiting the Caribbean coast is the Creole-style cuisine, which is characterised by coconut milk and spices. Many of the vegetables grown and eaten in the region are native to Africa. Yucca, ackee and breadfruit are common, along with the general Costa Rican favourite of plantains. Meat and fish are often cooked slowly in spiced coconut sauce, particularly for a 'rundown' (*rondón*) stew. Local drinks range from rum to herbal teas.

Surfers surveying the waves at Playa Manzanillo

Puerto Viejo de Talamanca

The village-sized but vibrant coastal town of Puerto Viejo serves as a gateway to the beautiful beaches along the southern Caribbean coast and the verdant Talamanca hills inland. The local people have recently been joined by waves of foreign expats, whose influence is felt in the town's cuisine and music. However, Puerto Viejo is still distinctively Caribbean and the buzzing nightlife is built on reggae music and open-air bars. There are accommodation options in town, while visitors looking for a quieter stay can head for hotels along the coast. Tours and excursions go to cacao plantations, botanical gardens, indigenous reserves and the Gandoca-Manzanillo refuge.

Refugio Nacional de Vida Silvestre Barra del Colorado

Barra del Colorado National Wildlife Refuge, which borders Nicaragua, consists of a remote marshy landscape teeming with wildlife. Even in comparison to the rest of the northern Caribbean region, Barra is hard to get to (flying is the best way) and around. Rivers, canals and lagoons break up the land, which is further saturated by abundant rainfall, so you can get around only by boat. Fishing is the main earner of the local community, and the lodges offer sport-fishing trips for guests. Those more interested in observing nature can paddle about in canoes or kayaks and expect to see countless birds as well as possibly some reptiles and mammals. There is a small ranger station near the village of Barra del Colorado, where admission fees are paid, but for tourist information head to Diana's Souvenirs, near the airport.

Refugio Nacional de Vida Silvestre Gandoca-Manzanillo

Gandoca-Manzanillo wildlife refuge is one of the lesser-known gems of the Caribbean coast. It was created to protect one of the country's few remaining coral reefs, located just offshore. Behind the postcard-perfect white-sand beaches is a diverse landscape of tropical rainforest, farmland and mangroves. Birds, including colourful parrots and toucans, are abundant, and watch out for tiny poison dart frogs while walking through the forest. At the time of writing there is no official entrance and no admission charge due to an ongoing administrative dispute, but you can access maps from the Minae office in Manzanillo village. Hiking in the refuge is rewarding because of the scenic beauty, but also challenging due to the inevitable mosquitoes and often extreme heat. Trails are not well marked, and hiring a local guide or booking an organised tour is likely to enhance and simplify your experience. A range of aquatic activities is available, including kayaking, sport-fishing and dolphin tours. Sea turtles nest on the beaches and it is possible for tourists to spend some time helping out with turtle protection efforts (*see p129*).

Reserva Indígena Cocles

Within the Talamanca region there are several indigenous reserves, home to Bribrí and Cabécar peoples, who have lived in the area since pre-Columbian times. The local grassroots organisation ATEC (*see p129*) arranges for tourists to visit some of the communities on a guided hiking or horseback tour. The reserve encompasses a large area of land from near Puerto Viejo up into the Talamanca Mountains and has about 200 inhabitants from the Bribrí and Cabécar groups.

Tortuguero

Colourful Tortuguero village has one of the most remote and scenic settings in the country, on a sliver of land at the northern edge of the national park, with the Caribbean Sea on one side, a canal on the other and rainforest all around. The village exudes a typically Caribbean charm. Brightly painted wooden houses with sloping zinc roofs break up the expanse of green, and numerous palm trees provide valuable shade from the hot sun. There are accommodation options in the village or you can stop by on a tour from one of the local lodges. Lots of guided boat tours and boats for independent hire are available, and there is also a grocery shop, bakery and several restaurants.

Bright buildings among palm trees in Tortuguero village

Tour: To Tortuguero from San José

This popular transfer route passes a series of scenic or interesting spots.

Many lodges in Tortuguero will pick you up from your hotel in San José and follow this route by coach and boat. The transfer takes about four hours. If travelling independently on a bus or by car you can stay on the road to further down the coast to board a boat at Moín (you may have to stay the night and leave the next morning due to early boat timetables).

1 Parque Nacional Braulio Carrillo

Soon after leaving San José the route passes through the picturesque wilderness of Braulio Carrillo National Park, with dense forest rising up on each side of the road.

The road winds its way to the small town of Siquirres, at which point the coach will turn off onto a smaller road. The best option for independent travellers is to stay on the main road to Moín, but you might choose to have a look at the banana plantation out of interest first.

2 Banana plantation

The small road traverses a vast banana plantation and is an interesting route for travellers to get a sense of working life in the region.

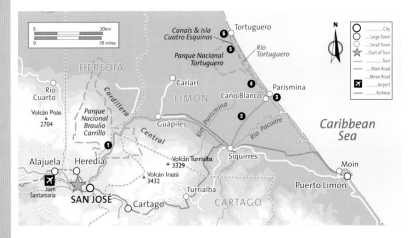

The road goes as far as Caño Blanco, which is across the river from the fishing village of Parismina, and your journey will now continue by boat.

3 Parismina

The small community of Parismina attracts visitors for two reasons, fishing and turtles: leatherback, green and hawksbill turtles all nest here. At the mouth of the Río Parismina the coastal wetland vegetation also provides a popular home for many wading birds. Look inland on a clear day and you will see the hazy but distinctive silhouette of Volcán Turrialba looming over the plain.

The boat turns into the Río Tortuguero (also known as Canal de Tortuguero) and begins to head northwest, separated from the Caribbean Sea by a thin strip of land.

Volcán Turrialba from the Río Parismina

4 Río Tortuguero

Keep looking out for waterbirds, which are abundant along the banks of this wide, calm river. At some points the surface of the water is blanketed by water lilies.

A short distance from Parismina the scenery shifts from agricultural plain to lush rainforest as you glide into the national park.

5 Canals

Several aquatic trails thread inland through the park from Río Tortuguero. The first of these, Caño Chiquero, branches off from the west bank of the river and leads to two others, Caño Mora and Caño Harold. To the east, parallel to the river, is one of the lagoons.

The boat glides around a small island (Isla Cuatro Esquinas), just before passing Tortuguero village, and at this point the river merges into the lagoons.

6 Tortuguero

Look out on the east bank of the lagoon for the houses of Tortuguero village, splashes of colour tucked away beneath tall palm trees. This is where the visitor centre for the park is located and where the one land trail begins.

Your tour may end at the village if you are staying here, or at one of the lodges along the sand bank.

Colourful creatures of the rainforest

Rainforest habitats teem with often diminutive but impressively colourful amphibians, insects and reptiles. Tropical forests are an ideal environment for frogs, and Costa Rica is home to a wide and fascinating assortment. The red-eyed tree frog, with its blue and yellow sides, orange feet and bright green body, is one of the most vibrantly coloured frogs in the world. These frogs are nocturnal and favour trees with big leaves, which they cling to during the day to sleep, tucking away their colours so that they camouflage perfectly. Although the rainforest is their natural habitat, they are also found on banana plantations. If threatened they can open their huge red eyes to startle the predator long enough to escape. Other interesting tree-dwelling frogs found in Costa Rica include Spurrell's flying frog, which cannot actually fly but paraglides from leaf to leaf, feet splayed. Descriptively named glass frogs have translucent skin, giving them an ethereal quality.

The rainforest floor is home to the diminutive poison dart frogs (just 1–5cm/⅓–2in in length), some of nature's most toxic creatures. The poisons produced by their skin were once used by indigenous peoples to coat arrows and darts, hence the name. Some of these distinctive frogs are vivid red with blue or black legs, while others are black and green. Their bright colours evolved as a form of protection, warning predators that they are poisonous.

In lowland watery forest areas such as Tortuguero you might come across a reptile such as an emerald basilisk lizard or dinosaur-like green iguana. Adult male green iguanas turn bright orange in the mating season (November–December).

Snakes are found throughout Costa Rica, but many favour lowland tropical forests. In total the country is home to 162 different species of snakes, of which 22 are venomous. The risk to visitors of encountering any of these in the wild is minimal, but it is always wise to watch your step when walking through the rainforest. The most dangerous snakes are the huge bushmasters (*matabuey*), which are native to mountainous and densely forested habitats, and the *fer-de-lance* or '*terciopelo*', which tend to favour

The morpho butterfly

rainy areas or river banks. Both of these are neutrally coloured and well camouflaged, but some poisonous snakes, such as the bright yellow eyelash pit viper and the striped red, black and yellow coral snake, are gaudy. Of course, you will not want to hang around admiring an example of this splendour should you come across one!

Butterflies are a far more innocent form of colourful creature, and numerous species flutter around Costa Rica's tropical forests. One of the best-known is the vivid blue morpho, which appears an unremarkable brown colour with its wings closed, but reveals an eye-catching flash of blue as it flies. Less commonly seen winged creatures include the shimmering blue and red blush butterfly and the extraordinary clear-winged butterfly. Diverse spiders also make their homes in the rainforest, which provides them with an abundant diet of insects, and spider webs link the tree trunks. On the forest floor, leafcutter ants conduct efficient nest-construction missions, and you may well encounter them as they cross the trails with their leaf fragments.

Southern Zone

Even by the high standards of a country famed for its natural wonders, the Southern Zone stands out as remarkable. This region contains several of the most remote spots in Costa Rica and a large proportion of the land is still an unspoilt wilderness. The terrain varies immensely, from the misty mountain peaks of the Cordillera de Talamanca to the coastal tropical rainforest and mangrove swamps on the Península de Osa and around the Golfo Dulce.

Southern Costa Rica holds many of the country's records: the highest mountain (Cerro Chirripó at 3,819m/12,529ft), the largest protected area (La Amistad International Park, which continues into Panama), the most isolated national park (Isla del Coco, 500km/310 miles from the mainland)

Bahía Drake Bay, as seen from above

and the last significant expanse of lowland rainforest on the Pacific coast of Central America (Corcovado National Park). Although the multiple charms of the Southern Zone do attract tourists, this is one of the least-visited parts of the country overall due to the inaccessibility of its most beautiful areas. Much of the Osa Peninsula is untouched by roads, while La Amistad and Chirripó parks are largely unexplored by visitors other than committed hikers.

Perhaps unsurprisingly, given the high density of well-preserved primary forest, wildlife is more plentiful and varied here than in all of Costa Rica, and since this is also one of the most sparsely populated regions you are likely to see more animals than people. There are a number of indigenous reserves located around the region, and some of the people who live here belong to the same groups as the earliest inhabitants thousands of years ago.

Bahía Drake

Drake Bay was named after the British pirate and explorer Sir Francis Drake, who landed here in 1579 and supposedly buried treasure somewhere nearby. It is tricky to get to, but rewarding, with stunning views out to sea. This is a distinctly marine destination, and attractions in the area include boat trips to Isla del Caño, scuba diving, kayaking, sport-fishing and whale-watching. More than 25 species of dolphins and whales have been spotted migrating through the area. Some of the lodges in the area are engaged in research and conservation as well as tourism, and they offer educational tours.

Casa de Orquídeas

Surrounded by the rainforest, this remote botanical garden is a secluded gem. As well as the orchids that gave the garden its name, the vibrant

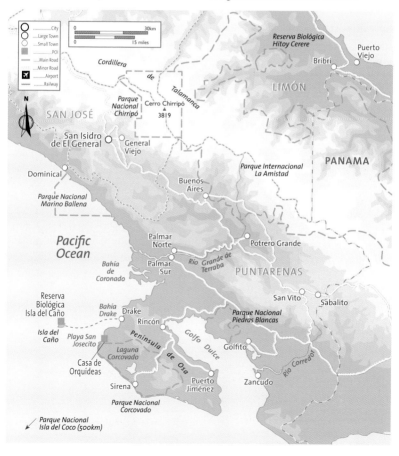

collection includes various tropical flowers, ornamental plants and fruit trees. Guided tours are offered. The garden can be reached on foot from the nearest lodges on Playa San Josecito or by boat from other lodges along the coast.

Dominical to Parque Nacional Marino Ballena

The small beach-side town of Dominical is a surfing destination, but it also makes a convenient base for visiting Parque Nacional Marino Ballena. The stretch of coastline to the south of town, much of which is protected within the park, is one of the loveliest in the country and encompasses beaches (sandy and rocky), river estuaries and mangrove

Whales in Parque Nacional Marino Ballena

swamps. Ballena also protects a section of the Pacific Ocean home to sea turtles, dolphins, breeding humpback whales and coral reefs. Despite all these attractions it receives few visitors and is one of the quietest national parks in Costa Rica. There are no hiking trails, but the golden beaches are perfect for a relaxing stroll, a spot of sunbathing and a dip in the sea. Boat tours and snorkelling are the main activities offered along this laid-back stretch of coast, and if you are lucky you may see some of the marine creatures. Humpback whales are not often spotted, although there is a chance in the months of August–October and December to April. There are convenient places to stay in the nearby tiny village of Uvita or between the village and the park. *Ranger station at Playa Bahía, Uvita. Tel: (506) 743 8236. Admission charge.*

Golfito area

Like Puerto Jiménez, Golfito, on the opposite shore of the Golfo Dulce, has a beautiful setting but little of interest to keep travellers, other than sport-fishers, in town. The forested hills behind the town are protected within a wildlife refuge. For a relaxing and remote beach break, head south to the little town of Zancudo, where there is a river estuary covered in mangrove swamps and a black-sand beach offering safe swimming and gentle surf conditions that are often suitable for beginners.

The 'whale fin' peninsula in Marino Ballena

Parque Internacional La Amistad

La amistad means 'friendship', and this vast park represents an important collaboration between Costa Rica and Panama to protect a shared natural treasure. In 1983 UNESCO declared the La Amistad-Pacífico Conservation Area (which comprises La Amistad, Chirripó National Park and several other national parks and reserves in the region of the Talamanca mountain range) a World Heritage Site. The varied wilderness of La Amistad is home to an impressive assortment of animals, including all six species of cats found in the country, Baird's tapirs and giant anteaters. There are five indigenous reservations within the park's borders. Travellers are advised to stay on the campsite at Altamira ranger station, which has the best facilities and from where there are hiking trails.

Park headquarters at Altamira.
Tel: (506) 200 5355. Admission charge.

Coastal rainforest in Parque Nacional Corcovado

Parque Nacional Chirripó

Mountainous Chirripó National Park features several lofty peaks, including Cerro Chirripó, the highest in the country at 3,820m (12,533ft). The landscape is a layering effect of *páramo* (high-altitude grassy moorland), glacial lakes, oak trees and cloud forest. Birds are abundant and this is a prime birdwatching destination. To visit Chirripó you need to book at least a day in advance both for park entrance, as visitor numbers are significantly restricted, and for accommodation at the hostel-style Crespones Base Lodge, the only place to stay in the park. You will need to bring all your own food and warm clothes as it gets cold at high altitude. The dry season (late December to April) is the best time to visit and the park is closed in May.

Ranger station. Tel: (506) 200 5348. Open: 6.30am–noon & 1–4.30pm. Admission charge (includes hostel).

Parque Nacional Corcovado

Corcovado (literally, 'hunchback') National Park is the only remaining extensive tropical humid forest on the Pacific coast of the isthmus and it is an amazing place, with a density and height of vegetation comparable to that of the Amazon basin. Some 500 different species of trees have been recorded, some of which are 50m (164ft) tall or more, and the eight distinct ecosystems include mangrove and palm swamps, primary rainforest and cloud forest. Identified inhabitants are 140 species of mammals, 367 species of birds, 117 species of amphibians and reptiles, 40 freshwater fish and a vast insect population comprising 6,000 species. In short, the park teems with wildlife, including some endangered or rare species such as the Baird's tapir, giant anteater, harpy eagle and jaguar. Unfortunately, Corcovado is plagued by poaching, which is endangering the jaguars by targeting peccaries, their main food source. This area has the largest population of scarlet macaws in Costa Rica, and you have a good chance of seeing these vibrant birds, particularly along the beaches near their favourite almond trees. Assorted other birds, all four species of monkeys found in the country and small mammals like coatis, are also fairly easy to spot.

Hiking in Corcovado is challenging, due to the heat and humidity, and is best attempted in the dry season (December to April) to avoid the worst of the mud. Unless you are travelling with a tour company or package arranged by a lodge, there is a fair amount of planning involved in visiting this remote park. Camping is allowed only at the *puestos* (ranger stations), where basic facilities are available for a small charge. The Sirena station also has dormitory accommodation and offers meals. It is necessary to make a reservation in advance to stay at any of the ranger stations, and it is also a good idea to hire a trained local guide to lead you along the trails.

Open: 8am–4pm. Admission charge. For lodging reservations, information and maps contact Oficina de Area Conservación Osa, Puerto Jiménez. Tel: (506) 735 5036/735 5580.

A crocodile lurks near a Corcovado river

Walk: Corcovado

This is the most popular route across Corcovado and can be done independently in a group of two or more, although going with a local guide is definitely recommended. It is a challenging hike of several days' duration, involving camping, and you need a reasonable level of physical fitness and to have acclimatised yourself to the jungle conditions in order to enjoy it. Travel as light as possible, but carry plenty of food and drinking water (you can refill bottles at ranger stations, but do not drink from streams or rivers). Also bring camping essentials, sunscreen, a compass, mosquito net and repellent. Dress for mud and heat.

Allow at least three days in total as you need a full day to hike from Los Patos to Sirena and a second full day for Sirena to Carate via La Leona.

Start at the small village of La Palma (if you are not staying at a nearby lodge you can reach the village by taxi from Puerto Jimenéz).

1 La Palma to Los Patos

It is 14km (9 miles) from La Palma to Los Patos ranger station. You should be able to get a taxi most of the way but will have to hike the last section inside the park (about 5km/3 miles). The trail meanders across the Río Rincón more than 20 times.

2 Los Patos to Sirena

This 18km (11-mile) trail is shady and offers a good chance of spotting wildlife. There is a picturesque waterfall near Los Patos and several more crossings of the Río Rincón. The first 6km (4 miles) is undulating, mainly in a downhill direction, but the rest of the trail is flat. You will pass Laguna Corcovado and the palm swamp, then cross the Río Sirena and the Río Pavo.

3 Around Sirena

Sirena Ranger Station, near the coast, serves as the park headquarters, and you are likely to meet researchers as well as other travellers while staying here. This is the best area for seeing mammals, such as tapirs, peccaries, agoutis, monkeys and possibly even a jaguar or ocelot (sometimes glimpsed in the small hours before dawn). A web

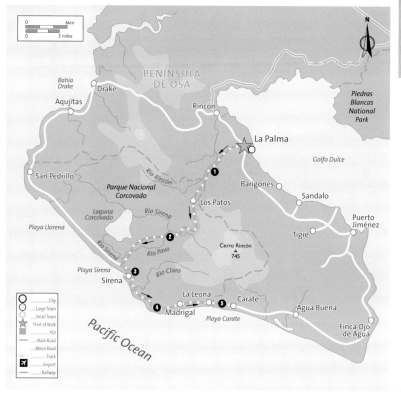

of short trails branches off from the station, including the interesting riverside Sendero Claro, home of aquatic birds and snails.

4 Sirena to La Leona

This is a hot 16km (10-mile) trek along wild sandy beaches and through coastal rainforest. You will need to wade across the Río Claro shortly after leaving Sirena; check details of tides with the rangers. Birds are a guaranteed sight and you are also likely to see small mammals including monkeys. Look out particularly for the distinctive scarlet macaws. You will also pass fascinating bat caves and waterfalls.

5 La Leona to Carate

After La Leona Ranger Station it is another 3.5km (2 miles) along the beach to Carate (about an hour's walk). Even after exiting the park you will still be walking through a picturesque landscape of dense rainforest laced with rivers where you might see caimans and crocodiles.
From Carate there is a collective taxi truck to Puerto Jiménez, which leaves in the evening (check locally for time).

Toucans are among the 367 species of birds living in Corcovado

Parque Nacional Piedras Blancas

Little-visited Piedras Blancas National Park protects a patch of mainly primary coastal rainforest located to the north of Golfito. Although less famous than Corcovado, Piedras Blancas, which was once an extension of the larger park, has equal beauty and exceptional biological variety. It has even been found that there is a higher diversity of trees within the 12,500ha (30,000 acres) of this park than anywhere else in the country. The park was created in 1992, adding an important link in an arc of protected land around the Golfo Dulce. At the time of writing, Piedras Blancas does not have visitor facilities, but it is possible to visit from the coastal lodges, which have trails extending into the forest. This really does seem like a tropical paradise, with deserted beaches fringed by the outline of towering forest and the sounds of the jungle all around.

Península de Osa and Golfo Dulce

'The most biologically intense place on Earth'; this frequently quoted accolade from *National Geographic* highlights the significance of the Osa Peninsula, an awe-inspiring landscape largely carpeted in dense rainforest. Corcovado National Park is the main reason visitors come here, but the beauty of the area extends beyond the park boundaries, north to gorgeous Drake Bay and across the scenic Golfo Dulce

('Sweet Gulf') to the beaches and protected forests lining the opposite coast. The Golfo Dulce is one of the deepest gulfs in the world and marine life is copious. Crossing the gulf in a small boat is an attraction in its own right, offering spectacular views of both coasts and sometimes sightings of the dolphins and whales which are drawn to the sheltered waters. Bottlenose, spinner and spotted dolphins are frequent visitors, while humpback whales migrate though the gulf in September. The conservation of the Osa area has not always been easy, particularly since the peninsula was historically rich in gold. The ancient Diquis people found abundant gold here, and in more recent years *oreros* (gold-miners) continued illegally panning within the boundaries of Corcovado until they were forcibly removed by police in 1986, although a few remain around the area.

Puerto Jiménez

The town of Puerto Jiménez has an enviable location, overlooking the Golfo Dulce and with the wilds of Corcovado National Park nearby. Small planes land just outside the town and boats glide to and fro across the gulf from the dock, the busiest feature of this sleepy town. Puerto Jiménez has a good selection of budget hotels (unusual in the Osa region), assorted restaurants and useful facilities such as a bank and tourist information office. Although few travellers linger in the town, its immediate surroundings are scenic and there are plenty of opportunities for

A plane lands at the Puerto Jiménez airstrip

Birds of Costa Rica

Among the many amazing statistics about Costa Rica is that it is home or seasonal home to 10 per cent of all known birds (about 850 species), which is more than the USA and Canada put together. There is such a wide range of climates and habitats within this small country that numerous different birds are able to make their home here. Some birds even migrate seasonally within Costa Rica, travelling between the cool mountains and the warm valleys, coasts or lowlands.

One of the most showy and famous birds is the resplendent quetzal, which has held great cultural and symbolic significance throughout Central America ever since the time of the Maya, who traded in its dazzling green feathers, and the Aztecs, who worshipped a deity named Quetzalcoatl ('Plumed Serpent'). Quetzals do not survive long in captivity and they have therefore also become symbols of freedom in more recent years. Lots of people visit Costa Rica's cloud forests hoping to see one of these birds, and a new national park in the Southern Zone has even been named after them. Quetzals are members of the trogon family, and while the other trogons are not quite as

A white-throated magpie jay in Guanacaste

spectacular, they are also colourful birds with distinctive long tails.

Classic tropical birds such as toucans and parrots live in the rainforests of the Pacific and Caribbean regions. Six species of toucans and various parakeets frequent these areas and you should have a good chance of seeing some of them. Sadly, macaws have suffered greatly as a result of poaching and loss of habitat. Green macaws are one of the most endangered species in Costa Rica, along with the harpy eagle, and it is rare to see them. Scarlet macaws, easily identified by their eye-catching primary coloured feathers, are often spotted on the Osa Peninsula and in Parque Nacional Carara, but rarely elsewhere. Macaws, like most parrots, live in monogamous couples and like to stay close to their birthplace.

Hummingbirds are widespread throughout the country, and many of the tourist attractions have designated hummingbird gardens where you can marvel at these unique miniature birds with big names like purple-throated mountaingem, coppery-headed emerald and violet sabrewing.

Costa Rica's coastal and river wetlands, notably Tortuguero, Caño Negro and Palo Verde national parks, are particularly rich in birdlife. The aquatic birds commonly found in

The scarlet macaw

these areas include herons, cormorants, kingfishers, snowy egrets and roseate spoonbills. Pelicans and frigate birds, both distinctive because of their pouches, can sometimes be spotted gliding over the sea along both coastlines. One of the most distinctive birds found in the country's watery landscapes is the sun bittern, which favours rivers in low-lying forested hills. These grey birds display black, gold and chestnut mosaic patterns, resembling eyes, when they spread their wings.

Given this wealth of brilliant birds, it is intriguing that the small, brown and unprepossessing yigüirro, also known as the clay-coloured robin or grey thrush, was chosen as the national bird of Costa Rica. The yigüirro sings at the beginning of the rainy season and is seen as a symbol of the fertility the rain will bring to the earth.

day trips. Chocolate-lovers should try the cacao farm Finca Köbö (*Tel: (506) 351 8576. www.kobofarm.com*), which offers guided tours in Spanish and English. Nearby beaches include Playa Platanes and Playa Blanca, both great for swimming, and Platanes also boasts a river with mangroves.

Reserva Biológica Isla del Caño

This uninhabited island reserve is the tip of a vast rock formation, the rest of which is underwater. Although Isla del Caño covers just a small area (3km by 2km/2 miles by 1 mile), it has cliffs soaring up to more than 100m (328ft) above sea level, presenting a distinctive silhouette from the mainland. You cannot visit independently, but the lodges around Bahía Drake usually offer day trips or you can book through a local tour operator. Diving and snorkelling are popular reasons to go, due to the fascinating underwater landscape of rock and coral and the abundant marine creatures which inhabit the protected waters offshore. Isla del Caño has a long history of receiving human visitors; it is thought that it was used by the Diquis as a burial site. They left behind a number of granite spheres, and several of these can be seen along a hiking trail through the forested interior of the island.

San Isidro

San Isidro is the biggest town in the Southern Zone and its location in the Valle de El General is scenic, fringed by the soaring mountain peaks of the Cordillera de Talamanca,

Some of the most beautiful parts of the Southern Zone are inaccessible by road

San Isidro is a good launch pad for hikes to Mount Chirripó

and convenient, next to the Interamericana road. San Isidro is the patron saint of farmers and animals, and life here is based around agriculture. The town has all the useful facilities for travellers: hotels, restaurants, banks and internet access. The area has beautiful countryside, an abundance of birds and farms open to visitors. A good example of the latter is Rancho La Botija, a working coffee and sugar farm with a boating lake and daily guided tours to a stone carved with pre-Columbian petroglyphs. The community-run Las Quebradas Biological Centre is another possible excursion and includes walking trails and a butterfly garden.

Rancho La Botija, Rivas.
Tel: (506) 770 2146/770 2147.
www.rancholabotija.com. Open:
Tue–Sun 8.30am–5pm (tours 9am).
Admission charge.
Las Quebradas Biological Centre.
Tel: (506) 771 4131. Open Tue–Sun
8am–4pm. Admission charge.

ISLA DEL COCO

The remote Isla del Coco, which floats more than 500km (310 miles) off Costa Rica's southwest coast, earned the nickname of 'Dinosaur Island' after an appearance in the opening scene of the film *Jurassic Park*. This was not Coco's first claim to fame; for centuries, legend had it that pirates had hidden treasure on the island, although numerous treasure hunts were unsuccessful. Today Coco is a national park, valued for the unique ecological treasures that have thrived in its luxuriant rainforest. Divers are motivated to make the long and expensive journey from the mainland, lured by the island's plentiful marine life, but illegal fishing has proved to be a real problem.

Indigenous Costa Ricans

Once upon a time the area that is now Costa Rica was populated by a number of tribal societies. Like the animals of the region, the people represented a meeting point of north and south. They traded with people from as far away as Mexico and Colombia, leading to diverse cultural influences. Each tribe was hierarchical, with a *cacique* (chief) at the top of the social structure and shamans accorded great importance. Although specific customs and beliefs varied between the groups, they shared a general inclination towards spirituality and ritualism, as well as a practical reliance on the land. Different groups revered different animals, but the jaguar was widely considered sacred. The native people generally respected their forest environments and practised natural healing using plants (they believed in a combination of medicine and magic). These principles have stood the test of time in some of the cultures and still endure today.

Columbus wrongly believed, on seeing some Talamancan people adorned with gold objects, that the area was rich in this precious metal. In truth, Costa Rica had relatively little gold compared to nearby countries, although the Diquis people of the Osa Peninsula did leave a rich legacy of elaborate gold objects. This same productive group also left intriguing monolithic spheres in the Diquis valley near the Pacific coast and on Isla del Caño.

Indigenous Costa Ricans display craft items

Visitors and Ticos dancing in San José

The arrival of the Spanish in the 16th century marked the beginning of centuries of first persecution, then marginalisation of native Costa Ricans, which has only recently begun to be addressed by the government. Until 1949 indigenous people did not even have citizenship rights. Today, many of the surviving native cultures and languages are endangered, and indigenous Costa Ricans account for only about 1 per cent of the country's population. Some of these people have integrated with mainstream society, while many others live on reservations (see p17).

There is a particular concentration of indigenous reserves in the south, from the southern Caribbean across the Talamanca Mountains to the Osa Peninsula. Groups in this region include the Bribrí, Cabécar, Boruca and Guaymí. The Guaymí of the southwest have preserved their language and kept their traditional way of life fairly intact. They live off the land in often very remote spots. The Bribrí and Cabécar groups mainly live in the Talamanca region and share a belief that the forest ecosystem was a gift from Sibö, their god of creation, and is to be protected and treated with respect. Both groups speak their native languages alongside Spanish, and the Bribrí in particular have adopted aspects of modernity without relinquishing their traditions. The Boruca are known for their cultural festivals, most notably the Fiesta de los Diablitos (see p20).

Further north, the Maleku people have also retained their ancient language and cultural heritage. Once renowned as jade sculptors, they now make various crafts such as jewellery and pottery, which they sell to travellers. The Chorotega people of the Nicoya Peninsula, who were also known for their jade work, did not survive the Spanish invasion, but their long-established civilisation left a legacy in the festivals and crafts of the region.

Getting away from it all

A holiday in Costa Rica is all about getting away from everyday life and spending time in beautiful natural environments. The destination guide features national parks and other scenic areas, from beaches to volcanoes. The entries below are a combination of places that are more removed from the main tourist areas, and activities that are either unusual or especially relaxing.

Boat trips

Getting out on the water can be a perfect way to unwind, and along Costa Rica's coastlines and rivers there are many different boat trips on offer. Below are just a few examples.

Catamaran cruises in Guanacaste

Even if you are staying in one of the busiest towns in the country, such as Tamarindo, there are ways to get away from it all for a few hours. Arguably one of the most effective is to take a sailing trip along the Pacific coast. To add an extra level of relaxation, choose a trip which is timed to be out on the water in the late afternoon. The characteristically spectacular sunsets take on an additional beauty when viewed from the ocean. Some boat trips also incorporate snorkelling (*see p148*) near a quiet beach.

Hot-air balloons provide stunning panoramic views over the landscape

Horse riding in the Arenal area

Gandoca-Manzanillo

In the tropical heat of the southern Caribbean coast, marine activities provide an opportunity to cool down. You can take a boat to the offshore reef at Punta Mona to snorkel, or further out to sea on a dolphin-observation trip. Both can be arranged at Aquamor Talamanca Adventures (*see p172*).

Golfo Dulce

Although it attracts many travellers, the 'Sweet Gulf' feels like a remote paradise of deserted rainforest-fringed beaches and warm sheltered waters. A great way to enjoy this beautiful seascape is to paddle along the coast in a kayak (many lodges have kayaks for use) or join an excursion in a small boat.

Hot-air ballooning

There can be few better ways to get away from it all than by drifting above the countryside in a hot-air balloon. Serendipity Adventures (*see p171*), the only ballooning company in Costa Rica, offers sunrise flights over the San Carlos plain. The pilots aim to get close to a patch of rainforest and dip down into the tree canopy for a unique perspective. You will also fly over a rural landscape of rivers, farms and sugar-cane fields and, if the sky is suitably clear, enjoy a stunning view of Arenal volcano.

Hot springs

After a long day of hiking, horse riding or otherwise exerting yourself in one of Costa Rica's volcanic areas, consider treating tired muscles to a soak in a hot spring. In the Arenal area there is a wide range of thermal resorts, which vary greatly in price and style. Balneario Tabacón (*13km/8 miles west of La Fortuna. Tel: (506) 319 1900. www.tabacon.com. Open: 10am–10pm*) is the ultimate in extravagant pampering. Besides a number of steamy pools, it has a thermal waterfall, Jacuzzis, slides, a cocktail bar and spa treatments. On clear nights the resort also boasts a great view of the volcano, which serves as a reminder that Tabacón is subject to Arenal's whim (the resort is sometimes closed if it looks risky). Opposite is Las Fuentes Termales (*Tel: (506) 460 2020. Open: 10am–10pm*), which is annexed to Tabacón but significantly cheaper and less glamorous.

If you are looking for something in between the two, try Eco-Termales

Take the frog's lead and rest a while at a thermal resort

(*5km/3 miles west of La Fortuna. Tel: (506) 479 8484. Open: 10am–9pm*). This resort is sophisticated without being showy. Visitors need to call ahead or ask at the next-door Hotel el Silencio del Campo to book an appointment for one of the four-hour slots, at 10am, 1pm or 5pm. Dinner is served during the 5pm slot (at an additional price). Further away, in the town of Ciudad Quesada, is Aguas Termales de la Marina (*Tel: (506) 460 1692*), a good budget option.

There are countless other thermal springs located around the region – ask locally for more information. In Parque Nacional Rincón de la Vieja some thermal springs are accessible from the Santa María entrance, with cold springs nearby for a Turkish bath effect. Some of the hotels in the area also have access

to hot springs. Nearby Volcán Miravelles, although dormant, still generates enough underground geothermal activity to fuel a number of hot springs resorts. These include Thermo Manía (*Tel: (506) 673 0233. Open: 8am–10pm*) and Yökö Hot Springs (*Tel: (506) 673 0410. Open: 7am–10pm*), both of which offer accommodation and food as well as inexpensive day passes. Thermo Manía is the biggest resort, with seven springs, waterslides, waterfalls and play and boating areas for children. Yökö has four thermal springs, a waterfall and waterslide.

Off the beaten track

Despite Costa Rica's popularity as a holiday destination, there are still some areas that are off the beaten track. A couple of quiet regions are detailed below, but you will also find that even in regions that are generally touristy there are small hideaways to be discovered. One of the best ways to get away from it all is to bed down in the forest at a nature lodge hideaway. Costa Rica excels in this type of accommodation and you will find them scattered around the country (*see p136*). The best lodges have an emphasis on sustainability and environmental friendliness as well as giving visitors a unique opportunity to be surrounded by nature and to feel far removed from civilisation without relinquishing its comforts. See directory section for recommendations.

Cordillera de Talamanca

The most southerly of the mountain chains encompasses a vast protected area in Parque Internacional La Amistad and neighbouring Parque National Chirripó, as well as several smaller national parks and reserves. This is a majestic landscape of mountains, glacial lakes and dense evergreen forest. Getting around this region requires significant planning and a lot of walking, and as a result vast parts of it remain largely 'undiscovered'.

Northern plains

From the Cordillera de Guanacaste to the Caribbean Sea, northern Costa Rica is a landscape of wide plains (*llanuras*). The most remote is the Llanura de Tortuguero, which can be accessed only by boat, and while Parque Nacional Tortuguero is popular with tourists, the rest of the plain is little-visited. The Refugio Nacional de Fauna Silvestre Barra del Colorado has a similar landscape to Tortuguero, but it is much more difficult and costly to visit and as a result sees far fewer visitors. If you have the resources and the inclination to get there you will be rewarded with incredible wildlife sighting opportunities.

To the east the Llanuras de San Carlos and the Llanura de los Guatosos cover an expanse of farmland, fruit plantations, rivers and patches of tropical forest largely unexplored by tourists. At the southern end of the San Carlos plain, near the town of Puerto Viejo de Sarapiquí, are the remote protected rainforest areas of Rara Avis and La Selva. La Selva is a research station, frequented mainly

Rainforest lodge in Corcovado

Getting away from it all

by biologists and students, but there is also some limited accommodation for casual visitors and guided day tours are offered. Although Rara Avis is harder to get to, it has more facilities for travellers. To visit the reserve you will have to stay at least one night, as it takes several hours to get there by tractor from the nearest town (Los Horquetas).

Volunteering opportunities and community tourism

Here are some suggestions for a holiday with a difference and an additional feel-good factor. Travellers can help protect sea turtle eggs and hatchlings, help out on an organic farm or get involved in conservation efforts in protected areas. Community-focused programmes have the added bonus of giving you a chance to experience local culture, and Spanish lessons are sometimes included. You will usually have to pay expenses and make a minimum time commitment, but the organisations listed below have been chosen because they offer short-term activities which you can incorporate into your holiday.

Travellers relaxing at sunset on the remote Golfo Dulce

Turtle conservation is an option for volunteers

Asociación Nacional de Asuntos Indígenas (National Association of Indigenous Affairs. *Tel: (506) 759 9100. www.anaicr.org*) is a grass-roots organisation concerned with sea turtle conservation in Gandoca-Manzanillo. Volunteers can help for a minimum of one week.

Asociación Salvemos las Tortugas de Parismina (Save the Turtles of Parismina. *Tel: (506) 710 5183. www.costaricaturtles.org*) arranges accommodation with a local family and holiday activities alongside volunteering opportunities.

Asociación Talamanqueña de Ecoturismo y Conservación (ATEC. Puerto Viejo. *Tel: (506) 750 0191/750 0398. www.greencoast.com/atec*) focuses on environmentally and culturally

sensitive tourism in the Caribbean and southern regions by organising a range of activities including visits to indigenous reserves and farms.

ASVO (Association of Volunteers Working in Protected Areas. Based in San José. *Tel: (506) 258 4430. www.asvocr.org*) sends volunteers to help with trail maintenance in national parks, turtle conservation and teaching English for a minimum of two weeks.

Cultourica (*Tel: (506) 249 1271. www.cultourica.com*) arranges accommodation in community-run lodges and a variety of guided trips (of a day or longer) to reserves and other attractions that are away from the main touristy areas.

El Encantado de la Piedra Blanca (also known as CODECE. *Tel: (506) 228 0183. www.codece.org*) is a community tourism project based in San Antonio de Escazú, near San José, which offers an opportunity for travellers to spend time with local families. You can visit an old-fashioned sugar mill, hike through a forest preserve, enjoy typical country-style food and drink and learn about local legends.

Finca la Flor de Paraíso is an organic farm, which operates a Spanish language school alongside volunteer programmes (*see p164*).

Fundación Corcovado (*Tel: (506) 297 3013. www.corcovadofoundation.org*) – invites volunteers to assist their conservation and community education projects for a minimum of two weeks, staying with local families.

When to go

The dry season (broadly December to April) is the most popular time to visit Costa Rica, with the week between Christmas and New Year and Semana Santa (leading up to Easter) being particularly busy. However, although the dry season does promise the most reliable weather conditions in many areas, the wet season has the significant advantages of fewer crowds and potential bargains. San José and the Central Valley experience conditions similar to a temperate spring year-round, albeit with varying degrees of rain.

Activity breaks

Surfers can be accommodated somewhere year-round, due to the diversity of the two coastlines. As a general guide, from late June to the end of the rainy season is the optimum time to surf on the Pacific coast, but the Caribbean coast experiences its best waves from November through May. Diving and snorkelling tend to be most rewarding during the dry season, when the water visibility is at its clearest. Sport-fishing in rivers and lakes varies depending on the location, so it is best to check ahead. Slow months for fishing in the Caribbean Sea are June and July, while for much of the Pacific, with the exception of the south, September to November is generally slow. Sea and river kayaking trips can be arranged year-round, although conditions on individual rivers vary. Windsurfing on Laguna de Arenal is dependably good between December and April, but should be avoided in September and

October. For hiking and cycling, travelling in the dry season is undoubtedly easier and more enjoyable.

Dry season

For most of the country the dry season lives up to its name; sunshine and warmth are practically guaranteed each day and temperatures can soar to above 30°C (86°F), particularly in the northwest. There are exceptions to this rule; the perennially humid southwest and the Caribbean coast are never without rain for long, while the cloud forest label speaks for itself. It is also worth bearing in mind that it can feel very chilly at high altitudes year-round. The dry season, called *verano* (summer) by locals, is certainly the best time for a classic beach break and also boasts the best driving conditions. However, the understandable popularity of these months means that many places get booked up early, prices are often higher and there is great pressure on many of the national parks. In addition, local schoolchildren are on holiday between December and February, meaning more crowds on the beaches.

Wet, or green, season

The rainy season is known locally as *invierno* (winter), but the ministry of tourism has created a new description of 'green season', which also applies. Between the months of May and November the popular spots are quieter and invigorated by the plentiful rain, so those who don't mind getting wet are likely to find this a more refreshing time to visit. These months also have the added advantage of discounts in many hotels, and it is not usually necessary to book so far in advance. June and July are gaining in popularity and are generally busier than the rest of the season. In September and October the rains are at their most intense, making it very difficult to travel in certain regions, particularly Nicoya. However, even at the height of the wet season it tends to rain only in the afternoons; mornings are sunny and pleasant.

WEATHER CONVERSION CHART

25.4mm = 1 inch

$°F = 1.8 × °C + 32$

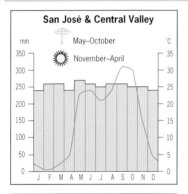

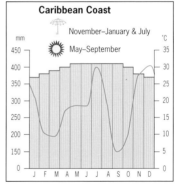

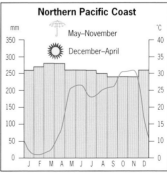

Getting around

Although Costa Rica is a relatively small country, journey times can be long, partly because there are a significant number of areas where roads are unpaved or completely non-existent. The mountain chains that form a physical divide between the two coasts complicate matters as well. There is a good infrastructure in the Central Valley area, and the Interamericana road traverses the entire length of the country in a winding line from northwest to southwest. Be prepared for an adventure in more remote areas, where boats and light aircraft are often the most practical, and sometimes the only, ways of getting around.

Boats

A sizeable section of the northern Caribbean region, stretching from Tortuguero National Park to the Nicaraguan border, can be accessed only by boat, as can some of the beaches and lodges around the Golfo Dulce. Even where boats are not the sole transport option they are often the most practical. Ferries cross the Golfo de Nicoya, and a short boat hop across the Laguna de Arenal is part of the quickest route between La Fortuna and Monteverde.

Buses

Costa Rica has a good network of public buses and these definitely represent the budget-travel option. As long as you are not in a hurry (local buses tend to be very slow) it is possible to travel from San José to almost anywhere in the country. However, other places are not so well interconnected and it is often necessary to change buses in the capital. At larger stops you can buy tickets in advance, and this is recommended at busy times or on popular routes. The government tourism office (Instituto Costarricense de Turismo, ICT) (*Tel: (506) 223 1733 ext 277. www.visitcostarica.com. Open: Mon–Fri 9am–5pm; closed for lunch*), which has offices at the Correo Central and in the Plaza de la Cultura in San José, provides bus schedules. Public buses do not have wheelchair access. The companies Interbus (*Tel: (506) 283 5573. www.interbusonline.com*) and Grayline (*Tel: (506) 220 2126. www.graylinecostarica.com*) run minibus services designed for tourists between the most popular destinations. These are significantly pricier than the local buses, but they are faster, more comfortable and very convenient as they pick you up at the hotel you are leaving and drop you off at your new hotel.

Domestic flights

The two internal airlines operating in Costa Rica are NatureAir (*Tel: (506) 220 3054, www.natureair.com*) and Sansa (*Tel: (506) 221 9414, www.flysansa.com*). Both airlines fly out of San José's Juan Santamaría airport, to destinations in the south, northeast and west of the country. They fly small aircraft (seating 14 or 19 passengers) and baggage is limited to 12kg (26lbs) per passenger. Excess baggage is generally carried at a charge, although the airlines officially reserve the right not to take it if flights are very full. This is certainly an exhilarating way to travel, and it is a practical option if you are heading for one of the more remote areas, such as Puerto Jiménez, which take a long time to reach by road.

Driving

There are significant complications with driving around Costa Rica: road signs are almost non-existent outside San José. Be prepared to get lost – allow plenty of time, take a map and learn enough Spanish to ask for directions. If possible, ask for directions at your hotel or a tourist office before you set out. Driving can also be challenging and risky due to dangerous drivers and the nature of the roads, many of which are unpaved, have steep bends and/or get very muddy during the rainy season. These factors all contribute to a

CAR RENTAL TIPS

- Be prepared to spend – it is not cheap.
- Guard against false accusations of damage by going through a Costa Rican travel agent or choosing a reputable firm. Check the car carefully for existing damage.
- In the high season it is best to reserve a car in advance. A number of international companies have branches in Costa Rica.
- Mapache (*Tel: (506) 586 6300. www.mapache.com*) and Toyota (*Tel: (506) 258 5797. www.carrental-toyota-costarica.com*) are recommended local companies. They both offer a car-and-driver service, which provides peace of mind by letting someone with good local knowledge do the driving.
- Opt for the full insurance – pricey, but worth it.

seriously high rate of road-traffic accidents. Always drive defensively. The speed limit, unless otherwise indicated, is 40kph (25mph) in urban areas and 60kph (37mph) elsewhere.

Taxis

Taxis are a common form of transport throughout most of the country and can be hired for long trips as well as short journeys around towns. Licensed taxis (which are red, marked with yellow triangles) have meters for short trips, but if hiring for a longer trip you need to agree the fee in advance. Walking at night is generally not advisable, for a variety of reasons – from snakes crossing roads to personal safety – so if you are going out, it is a good idea to ask the place you are travelling from to call you a taxi.

Getting around

Accommodation

Tourism is a well-established industry in Costa Rica and there is an extensive choice of hotels ranging from small budget options to expensive resorts. More unusual options include staying in a lodge in the rainforest or on a working cattle ranch. Hotels are rated by the government's 'Green Leaf' programme, which looks at sustainable development, environmental friendliness and cultural-social awareness.

The high season for accommodation coincides with the dry season (usually December–April, although this varies throughout the country). Many places raise their prices for the week between Christmas and New Year and the week before Easter (Semana Santa) and lower them during the rainy season. It is advisable to book well in advance if visiting during high season. There is a hotel tax (currently 16.39 per cent), which may or may not be included in the advertised price, so check the small print.

Boutique and luxury

Although many of the hotels in the more indulgent price bracket are part of international chains, there are also numerous boutique hotels and unique

Luxury beachside hotel pool at Bahia del Sol

Gardens and pool at Mawamba Lodge

establishments. The group 'Small Distinctive Hotels of Costa Rica' features six places that offer a combination of luxury and originality. Boutique hotels are found in various settings around the country, from coffee plantations to beaches, but they share a preoccupation with aesthetic loveliness. These hotels are not cheap, but they are generally worth the money if you are looking for somewhere special to stay.

Budget options

There are numerous low-priced hotels and some hostels around the country catering for travellers on a budget. Facilities vary widely, as does the availability of hot water, although in the hottest parts of the country you really will not miss it. Many places described as *cabinas* (cabins) are in the budget range, as are *hospedajes, albergues* and *posadas* (all of which translate loosely as 'lodgings'). Look for cheap lodgings in towns near popular national parks (e.g. Golfito, Quepos, Santa Elena, Tortuguero village). Ask to see rooms before you commit and check that they seem secure.

Camping

Many of the national parks have campsites, although in others camping is not permitted so always check in advance. Beach towns often have private campsites as well. Basic facilities (toilets, drinking water, cooking grills) are available at the campsites, but stock up on everything else you will need in

A beautifully crafted cabin at Playa Nicuesa Rainforest Lodge

advance as many are located in remote areas. Be kind to the environment by taking all rubbish away with you and using biodegradable products. Mosquitoes are present in their droves in the hot humid forest areas, making insect repellent an essential item.

Farms and ranches

Several tour operators and co-operatives arrange for travellers to stay on *fincas* (small farms) or in community-run rural lodges. Some of these are listed in the 'Getting away from it all' section (*see p129*). In Guanacaste, a number of *haciendas* have been extended to include hotels on the same sites as the working cattle ranches.

Nature lodges

Wilderness lodges are one of Costa Rica's specialities and they are ideal for travellers who want to be surrounded by nature in beautiful, remote settings, but still enjoy creature comforts such as private bathrooms with hot showers and big beds enveloped in mosquito nets. Lodges vary in price, but most are in the mid-range to top-end brackets. They tend to be located in hard-to-reach rainforest areas, such as Tortuguero and the Golfo Dulce, so they will generally arrange pick-ups for their guests, plan daily activities and serve all meals on site.

Self-catering

Self-catering is not as widespread as other accommodation options, but it can be found. Some hotels include big family suites, cabins or apartments with equipped kitchens. Even small village communities generally have a *pulpéria* (grocery store), although self-catering is undoubtedly easier in larger towns where there is better shopping.

Staying in a family home

Language schools often arrange for students to stay with local families to accelerate Spanish-learning as well as giving the student an opportunity to experience Costa Rican culture. If this appeals to you, there are a number of schools offering week-long courses, which could be combined with a holiday, as well as longer options

(try *www.languageschoolsguide.com/ CostaRica.cfm* for course listings). Organisations catering to travellers who want the home-stay without the lessons are less common, but there are a few. Bell's Home Hospitality (*Tel: (506) 225 4752. www.homestay.thebells.org*) arranges for travellers to stay at host homes in the San José area. Monteverde Homestays (*Tel: (506) 645 6627. www.monteverdehomestasy.com*) does the same near the cloud forests of Monteverde and Santa Elena. Bear in mind that you will need to be able to speak enough Spanish to communicate with your hosts.

Infinity pool at the El Parador in Manuel Antonio

Food and drink

The cocina típica *(typical cuisine) of Costa Rica is rustic and hearty, based on staples of rice, beans, meat or fish and plantains. There are interesting variations between the regions and international influences have added extra diversity. The tropical location yields an abundance of fruit, while beer and a sugar-cane spirit called* guaro *are the most typical drinks.*

Drinking

Costa Rica is synonymous with excellent coffee, which is the nation's favourite drink. Typical soft drinks include *refrescos* (refreshing fruit drinks) and herb teas. There is a huge import tax on alcohol so it is best to go for locally produced options. Beer tends to be the beverage of choice and local brands Imperial, Bavaria, Pilsen and Rock Ice are all reasonably priced. The Costa Rican spirit speciality is *guaro*, which is derived from sugar cane. This is strong stuff but good in lemony cocktails. Rum is also quite popular, particularly in the Caribbean region, and there are several good Costa Rican varieties as well as the

A squirrel enjoys some fresh local melon

Mono Azul Hotel Restaurant, a true 'rainforest café'

Nicaraguan brand Flor de Caña. Café Rica is a smooth, creamy coffee-based liqueur.

Alcohol is banned from sale on election days and at Easter to make sure everyone remains suitably sober.

Restaurants and eating out

The main meal of the day is typically eaten around noon, while dinner is generally at about 7pm. *Sodas*, which are small informal eateries found everywhere, serve cheap and hearty breakfasts and lunches, such as *gallo pinto* and *casados*, but are not usually open for dinner. *Restaurantes* are generally more formal than *sodas*, although prices and menus vary widely. There is a good selection of restaurants in San José and touristy areas, including plenty of international

options. Restaurants add tax (13–15 per cent) and service (10 per cent) charges to the bill, so there is no need to tip. Menus are generally available in English as well as Spanish. Various snacks ranging from fresh fruit to fried chicken can be bought from street vendors or from *soda* counters. Cooked bar snacks called *bocas* can make up a tasty tapas-style meal.

Shopping and markets

Markets are a treasure trove of exotic fruits and a good source of fresh food. Farmers' markets (*ferias*) are generally held on Saturday mornings, but many street and covered markets open daily (typically excepting Sundays) from dawn to early afternoon. Even small villages usually have a *pulpería* (grocery store), and bigger

Fruit for sale in Monteverde

towns have supermarkets, which tend to open long hours.

Specialities and highlights

An extensive range of tropical fruits includes *pejibaye* (a relative of the coconut with a nutty flavour, which is almost entirely unique to Costa Rica), *carambola* (star fruit), *granadilla* (passion fruit), *guayaba* (guava) and *mamones chinos* (a little like lychees but sweeter). More familiar fruits such as bananas, pineapples, oranges and grapefruit are in abundant supply too. The dish most frequently considered emblematic of Costa Rica is the traditional breakfast *gallo pinto* (*see box, right*). A typical lunch is the *casado* (literally 'married person'), a plate of meat or fish with rice, coleslaw salad and sometimes also fried plantains. Another

speciality is *tamales*, plantain-leaf wraps generally filled with maize flour, chicken or pork, raisins, chillies and olives.

The Caribbean and Guanacaste regions have their own distinct dishes. On the Caribbean coast these include the Creole staples of coconut milk, plantain chips and spices. A sweet delicacy is *pan bon* (glazed bread served with fruit and cheese). In Guanacaste the indigenous people of long ago left a culinary legacy, and the cowboy culture has also had an influence. Specialities include *chorreados* (corn pancakes), *rosquillas* (corn doughnuts) and *horchata* (a hot rice- or corn-based drink flavoured with cinnamon).

Vegetarians

Although vegetarians are a rarity among Ticos, the predominance of rice

GALLO PINTO

Typical breakfast dish *gallo pinto* ('spotted rooster') is simple but delicious. Rice, black beans, onion and fresh coriander are the staple ingredients. Sweet peppers, celery and garlic are also often added. For sauce Ticos use *salsa Lizano*, but a good substitution is a combination of Worcestershire sauce and a little Tabasco. Start by cooking the black beans according to packet instructions. Sauté dry rice with garlic and some chopped onion, pepper and coriander, add water and cook (alternatively you can use leftover cooked rice). Stir rice and beans together and sauté with some more onion, pepper, celery and coriander. Add sauce to taste. Serve with sour cream or eggs (scrambled or fried).

and beans means visiting veggies are relatively well catered for. Happily, specialities like *gallo pinto*, *sopa negra* (black bean soup) and plantains enable non-carnivores to sample local dishes. Many restaurants have a meat-free version of the traditional *casado* on their menus, and those that don't are generally happy to prepare one on request. In San José and the more touristy towns, notably Monteverde, there is a choice of restaurants that are entirely vegetarian or have a vegetarian menu. The situation is trickier for vegans, but manageable.

Food and drink

Typical Costa Rican food, suitable for vegetarians

Entertainment

Entertainment in Costa Rica largely revolves around music, dance and a programme of festivals and fairs throughout the country. In San José and some other towns and cities going to the theatre is another popular pastime. The Tico Times (www.ticotimes.net) has a 'weekend' section with events listings, and the most widely distributed daily newspaper, La Nación *(www.nacion.co.cr), also carries entertainment listings.*

The free publication *Guía de Ciudad*, available from the tourist office in San José, has listings of events in the capital, or you can check online at *www.entretenimiento.co.cr*. In rural areas, nightlife is often limited to torch-lit nature walks or a few cocktails at the hotel bar before an early night so that you can be up to make the most of the next day.

Bars and dancing

The most prominent and varied nightlife scene is, as you would expect, in San José, where it is easy to find somewhere to drink and dance the evening away. As a general guide, avoid the centre of town (which has an unfavourable reputation) and opt instead for the university district of San Pedro and Los Yoses or for the Centro Comercial El Pueblo near Barrio Amón. Fridays and Saturdays tend to be livelier than other nights, but most bars are open throughout the week. There is often a cover charge but rarely a strict dress code. Take a photocopy of your passport for ID.

Outside the capital, the situation is varied, from small towns with just a local bar to touristy areas like

Key Largo bar, San José

The piano bar at the Flamingo Bay Resort

Manuel Antonio where you will find a selection of venues serving cocktails to holidaymakers. Karaoke is very popular with Ticos and so is dancing, generally to music with a Latin rhythm. There are some seedy bars about, particularly in the larger towns and ports such as Puerto Limón and Puntarenas, but these tend to be obvious and hence easily avoided.

Cinema

Costa Rica does not have a film industry to speak of; cinemas in San José and the larger towns show Hollywood and other international films. English-language films are usually shown with Spanish subtitles, although they are sometimes dubbed (*hablado en español*), so it is best to check before buying a ticket. There are large modern multiplexes in the San José suburbs of Escazú and San Pedro. An example is the Cines del América (*see p162*) in the Mall San Pedro. In the centre of the city, Sala Garbo (*see p162*) features art-house films.

Festivals

Fiestas and *expo-ferias* (a combination of country-style fairs and cultural entertainments) are held throughout the year and throughout the country. They range from religious processions to colourful carnivals. *See* 'Background' (*pp20–1*) for a list of major events. If you are in Costa Rica around Christmas you will notice a real festival atmosphere. Fireworks are common and San José is transformed by the Festival de Luz parade shortly before Christmas and the week-long Las

Fiestas de Zapote carnival afterwards. For other carnivals, visit Puerto Limón in the week leading to 12 October for a vibrant street party with flamboyant parades, fireworks, fairground games, children's theatre, music and dancing, or Puntarenas in late February for a week of parades and fireworks.

Horse parades in Guanacaste

Festivals based around *topes* (horse parades) are a major feature of the Guanacaste calendar and a great opportunity for travellers to sample the local culture of this unique region. Although the *topes* are the centrepiece of the events, they are not the only entertainment on offer. There are also Costa Rican-style *recorridos de toros* (bull fights), which differ from the Spanish version in the important regard that the bulls are not killed. Dances, including the traditional Punto Guanacasteco, are another element of the festivals. Look out for the women dancers' billowing skirts, designed to represent ox-cart wheels. Food and drink stalls keep festival-goers nourished and cattle auctions often add a practical angle. Guaranteed dates for *topes* are Semana Santa, Guanacaste Day (25 July) and the week between Christmas and New Year, but they are held on other days as well so ask around locally.

Live music

Many bars have live music in various styles on certain nights of the week. You might also experience some live music

The Teatro Mélico Salazar in San José

in a restaurant or even be serenaded, particularly in Guanacaste where musicians playing traditional *marimba* instruments (accompanied by guitars and maracas) often feature in an evening's entertainment. If you find yourself in the Puerto Viejo de Talamanca area in March or April, check out the South Caribbean Music and Arts Festival, which takes place at the weekends. The emphasis is very much on local talent, with musicians and dancers showcasing the Caribbean musical tradition of calypso and reggae. There are also screenings of Costa Rican films.

For a completely different style, try the Monteverde Music Festival, a selection of predominantly jazz, folk and Latin music concerts held between late January and early April. Classical music fans could head to the small historic town of Barva, near Heredia, in July or August for the International Music Festival hosted by Austrian-style Hotel Chalet Tirol.

Staged performances

San José is the cultural centre for drama, dance and classical music performances. Plays are generally in Spanish, with the notable exception of the Little Theatre Group (*see p34*), which puts on several English-language plays a year, often at the Teatro Eugene O'Neill in Escazú. Non Spanish-speakers can also enjoy dance or musical productions. The Teatro Nacional (*see p34*) hosts performances

Beautiful interior at the Teatro Nacional

by the Compañía de Lírica Nacional (National Lyric Company, Costa Rica's only opera company) from June to August and by the Orquestra Sinfónica Nacional (National Symphony Orchestra) from April to December. Among the programme of performances at the Teatro Mélico Salazar (*see p34*) is the interesting Fantasía Folklórica, a medley of traditional music and dance from Guanacaste on Tuesday evenings. The Compañia Nacional de Danza (National Dance Company) also performs at Mélico Salazar.

Shopping

Normal shopping hours are 8am–6pm Monday to Saturday, although some shops open on Sunday and close on Monday and there may be lunchtime closures. Shops in popular tourist areas sometimes stay open later.

Alcohol and coffee

For all the coffee-lovers you know (and perhaps yourself) a packet of freshly ground beans is sure to make a great souvenir. Coffee is sold practically everywhere, from supermarkets to

Mercado Artesanal, San José

plantations (where you can also take a tour and sample different varieties). There is such an array available that it is easy to feel spoiled for choice, but the main advice to heed is to make sure you buy export quality brands as some of the coffee on sale for the domestic market is pre-sweetened. Reliable brands include 1820, Café Britt and the Tres Generaciones of the well-known Doka Estate (*see p48*). For coffee with a conscience try the organic, fair-trade Café Monteverde, which is produced by a co-operative. *Guaro* (*see p138*) is a uniquely Costa Rican alcoholic souvenir, and a large bottle of Cacique (the main brand) can be purchased in supermarkets or at the airport at bargain prices.

Craft items and souvenirs

Typical Costa Rican crafts include an array of wooden items, such as bowls, jewellery boxes and figurines, jewellery, ceramics and replica ox-carts. The hand-crafted tropical hardwood

Colourful sarongs for sale in Manuel Antonio

objects are lovely, but to promote the protection of the rainforest, opt only for those that have been made using sustainable tree farming methods. Biesanz Woodworks in Escazú (*Tel: (506) 289 4337. www.biesanz.com. Open: 8am–5pm Mon–Fri*) sells pricey but beautiful items made from specifically grown wood. The Kids Saving the Rainforest shop at Mono Azul Hotel in Manuel Antonio (*see p166*) is another good choice.

Traditional Chorotega-style pottery, including plates and vases, can be bought in the Guanacaste region, particularly in the town of Guaitíl (*see p68*). Artisans at some of the indigenous reserves make and sell decorated vases and bowls carved from gourds, painted wooden masks and wall hangings, among other items. The Monteverde–Santa Elena area is particularly good for shopping, with a range of gallery-shops featuring unique art works, crafts and jewellery. Jewellery replicating pre-Columbian jade or gold adornments makes a popular souvenir, and the obligatory range of T-shirts

and trinkets can be found in gift shops at tourist attractions and the airport.

San José

San José has a wide range of shopping options, from multilevel complexes to small crafts boutiques and markets. The Centro Comercial El Pueblo has restaurants and bars alongside souvenir and artisan craft shops, several of which stay open well into the evening for before or after-dinner shopping. Try the Mercado Artesanal for an enjoyable browse of multiple stalls selling handmade wooden items and various other souvenirs. There are several bookshops along the Avenida Central as well as scattered around the city, where you can pick up English-language fiction and books about Costa Rica.

WHAT NOT TO BUY

Avoid anything made from animal products or coral. Objects made from turtle shells, furs such as ocelot or jaguar and feathers from endangered bird species are actually illegal, although they are sold by some market traders.

Sport and leisure

Whether you are looking for an action-packed holiday or just a few activities to fill an otherwise relaxing break, you will find plenty to keep you occupied in Costa Rica.

Cycling

Provided you exercise significant caution (factoring in speeding drivers) and plan your route carefully, cycling through the beautiful landscapes of Costa Rica has the potential to be an exhilarating experience. Mountain bikes are the most practical option and can be rented throughout the country. However, road conditions in many places, such as Monteverde, make cycling more strenuous than enjoyable.

Diving and snorkelling

Isla del Coco (*see p121*) is considered the most spectacular dive site, but due to its remoteness it is only for serious and experienced scuba divers. Isla del Caño (*see p120*), near Bahía Drake, and Islas Murciélago and Santa Catalina in Bahía Santa Elena are more accessible. Courses, trips and equipment hire can be easily arranged in Bahía Drake and the northern Nicoya beach resorts. Water visibility is often low along the Pacific coast, but there is an abundance of marine life, including dolphins, whales, rays, sharks, turtles and tropical fish. The Caribbean diving centres of Puerto Viejo de Talamanca (*see p102*) and Manzanillo (*see p95*) offer a completely different experience, which is generally well suited to beginners. The water is often clearer and you will see coral reefs and colourful fish. Beginner scuba divers should consider taking a course, as these are reasonably priced in Costa Rica. Snorkelling is possible at many beaches, and trips can be arranged along both coasts. Gandoca-Manzanillo, Parque Nacional Marino Ballena and parts of northern Guanacaste are particularly popular destinations.

Football

Futból, the national sport of Costa Rica, is very popular among Ticos and you will see football pitches everywhere you go. Local teams are avidly supported, as is the *selección nacional* (national selection), often referred to as La Sele.

Horse riding

Horse riding has become a very popular leisure activity for travellers throughout the country, but particularly in Guanacaste and the Northern Zone. Horseback tours are a unique way to experience the countryside and reach some of the more inaccessible areas. Be sure to choose a reputable company though, and make full use of the safety equipment provided. Sadly, there have been reports of horses being mistreated and it is important to make sure you ride only on well-cared-for horses.

Kayaking and rafting

With so many waterways throughout the country, varying from tumbling white-water rapids to flat canals, there is as much scope for flexibility in kayaking and rafting as in walking and hiking. White-water rafting is very popular and numerous operators arrange trips. While this exhilarating activity is generally very safe, there is an obvious risk factor so it is important to make sure you choose a good company and a river that is suited to your level of experience. The Pacuare and Reventazón rivers, accessible from the town of Turrialba (*see p52*), are the most popular and also among the most challenging.

Sport-fishing

Costa Rica has become a popular sport-fishing destination, although this activity is usually prohibitively expensive and chosen only by real enthusiasts. The important distinction of the sport from regular fishing is that most of the fish are returned to the sea alive. There is good fishing along both coasts and some rivers. Golfito (*see p110*), Quepos (*see p62*), Playa Flamingo and Barra del Colorado (*see p102*) are particularly popular bases. The *Tico Times* features a column by a local fishing expert, advising anglers on the best places to go.

Surfing and windsurfing

There is good surfing along both coastlines, with plenty of variety to suit all levels. Beginners can take lessons at most of the popular surfing beaches, including Tamarindo, Jacó and Puerto Viejo de Talamanca. Laguna de Arenal (*see p86*) is undoubtedly the best place to windsurf in Costa Rica and it is also considered to be among the global best. The winds blowing across the lake are consistently good, but the water is chilly at 18–21°C (64–70°F).

Walking and hiking

In a country with so many national parks and reserves, walking is an obvious activity for travellers. Enthusiasts of long hikes, often involving camping, should head for the big wilderness areas such as Corcovado (*see p112*), Santa Rosa (*see p74*) and Chirripó (*see p112*) national parks, or the sprawling La Amistad (*see p111*) international park. Many of the parks have trails designed for shorter hikes of a day or just a few hours. Wherever you are walking, remember to carry plenty of water and protect against the sun.

Children

With its wealth of natural treasures combined with its safety and the friendliness of its people, Costa Rica makes an appealing and interesting destination for families. Between stunning tropical forests, sandy beaches and simmering volcanoes there are plenty of adventures to keep young visitors entertained. It's generally safe to travel around the country with children, although parents should seek medical advice regarding vaccinations for young children.

Around San José

Children are most likely to remember their trip to Costa Rica for the exciting outdoor activities, but the interactive Museo de los Niños (*see p30*) in San José is worth exploring. Parque Nacional de Diversiones (*tel: (506) 242 9200*) is an amusement park in the capital's La Uruca suburb. It includes the Pueblo Antiguo (old village), a re-creation of traditional houses featuring theatre events with actors in period costumes.

Beaches

Many of the beaches in Costa Rica, although beautiful, are not ideal for swimming. Riptides (*see p59*) are a serious potential risk to swimmers and in certain areas sharks are present. Despite this, however, there is still a good range of safe beaches where children can play happily in the sand and sea. Pretty Playa Sámara (*see p79*) has some of the gentlest waves on the Nicoya Peninsula. The idyllic white-

sand beaches of Isla Tortuga (*see p56*) are perfect for swimming, and children can also enjoy spotting marine wildlife on the boat trip over. Other beaches where it is safe to swim include Conchal (*see p67*), Punta Uva (*see p95*) and Manuel Antonio (*see p60*). Always check local advice.

Nature and national parks

For a truly educational and fascinating experience, try discovering a national park in the company of a trained guide. Children will benefit from the opportunity to learn all about the animals and plants they see. Costa Rica's wildlife sanctuaries are sure to delight young visitors, as is the hummingbird garden at La Paz (*see p42*); Manuel Antonio (*see p58*) is a good place for children to experience the rainforest. For a more general introduction to the biodiversity of Costa Rica, visit family-friendly INBioparque (*see p41*). In addition to a 3.5km (2-mile) walking trail, the

Bosque Eterno de los Niños (Children's Eternal Rainforest, *see p82*) has a children's nature centre and a tree nursery, where curious young visitors (and adults) can learn about conservation.

Restaurants

Costa Rican restaurants are typically welcoming to families with small children. Some have specific children's menus and those that do not are often willing to adapt meals on request.

Sport and leisure activities

Most activity operators welcome children to join in and will make adjustments where necessary. Age restrictions vary, but as a general guide children under six are often considered too young for a lot of activities. Older children may well be more adventurous than adults and might enjoy the zip-line canopy tours available in many areas. Many hotels and tour companies near rivers offer kayaking excursions or safari floats (rafting designed for wildlife-spotting rather than adrenaline rushes). Water babies might also enjoy the family-oriented leisure resort Ojo de Agua (*see p163*), just south of Alajuela. The resort is based around natural springs and has swimming pools and a boating lake.

Children

Children at INBioparque

Essentials

Arriving and departing

Air

Juan Santamaría (SJO), located just outside San José, is Costa Rica's main international airport. Daniel Oduber (LIR), near Liberia, receives some international flights and at the time of writing there were expansion plans. Many air travellers arrive from or via the USA, although there are a few direct flights from Canada (Toronto) and Europe, notably Madrid. There are also daily flights from Mexico City and several other Central and South American cities. There are no direct flights from the UK, Australia or New Zealand. The following national carriers serve Costa Rica:

American Airlines *Tel: 506 257 1266. www.aa.com*

Air Canada *Tel: 514 393 3333 (in Canada). www.aircanada.ca*

America West *Tel: 480 693 6718 (in the USA). www.americawest.com*

Continental *Tel: 506 296 4911. www.continental.com*

COPA *Tel: 506 222 6640. www.copaair.com*

Cubana de Aviación *Tel: 506 221 7625/5881. www.cubana.cu*

Delta *Tel: 506 256 7909. www.delta.com*

Grupo TACA *Tel: 506 296 0909. www.taca.com*

Iberia *Tel: 506 257 8266. www.iberia.com*

KLM *Tel: 506 220 4111. www.klm.com*

Lacsa see Grupo TACA

Martinair *Tel: 31 20 60 11 767 (in the Netherlands). www.martinair.com*

Mexicana *Tel: 506 295 6969. www.mexicana.com*

SAM/Avianca *Tel: 506 233 3066. www.avianca.com*

United Airlines *Tel: 506 220 4844. www.united.com*

US Airways *Tel: 800 011 0793/4114. www.usairways.com*

Land

San José is well connected to other Central American capitals by an international bus network (*www.ticabus.com*). Crossing the borders is straightforward as long as you have the necessary paperwork (check the requirements for the other countries). It is more complicated and expensive to drive across the borders independently. Make sure your vehicle is in good condition and includes a toolbox of spare parts and that you have all the necessary paperwork. Costa Rica does not charge travellers to enter the country, but there is a fee for vehicles, and drivers may have to pay road tax and local insurance.

Sea

Arriving by sea is not really a practical option, but some cruise ships make brief stops at Costa Rican ports, generally Caldera on the Pacific coast near Puntarenas, or Puerto Limón in the Caribbean.

Customs

Limits are imposed on importing cigarettes (maximum 500) and wine or spirits (maximum 3 litres). Photographic equipment is also subject to restrictions. Visitors are entitled to bring two still and/or video cameras and six rolls of film. It is illegal to buy or export any items covered under the Convention on International Trade in Endangered Species, such as tortoiseshell, certain bird feathers and furs, or any archaeological artefacts.

Electricity

All plug sockets are American two-pin style, so visitors wishing to use appliances with UK or continental plugs will need to bring adaptors and ensure that equipment is suited to 110 volts AC.

Money

Costa Rica's currency is the colón (plural 'colones'), but US dollars are widely used. Generally, visitors will use dollars to pay for large amounts (e.g. accommodation) and colones for smaller amounts (e.g. taxis), but it is possible to pay for most things in either currency. Colones are not available outside Costa Rica, so it is best to arrive with dollars and get some colones at an ATM (*cajero automático*). You can withdraw cash using debit cards with international symbols, although not all banks accept these. Major credit cards are generally accepted at hotels and restaurants (Visa and MasterCard most widely).

Opening hours

The day starts early in Costa Rica. Opening hours for national parks and other attractions vary, but 8–8.30am is a fairly common opening time and last admission is often before 5pm (sometimes as early as 3.30pm). Some of the parks and reserves offer tours after dark and some open at dawn. Many attractions close on Mondays. Banks are generally open on weekdays between 9am and 3pm.

Passports and visas

Passport holders of certain countries, including Canada, UK and USA, can stay in Costa Rica for up to 90 days without a visa. Citizens of Australia, Ireland, New Zealand and South Africa, among others, can stay for up to 30 days without a visa. Other travellers will need to obtain a visa from a Costa Rican embassy or consulate. You should carry a photocopy of your passport with you while in the country. The above rules apply to adults and to children travelling with both parents. A child accompanied by one parent can stay only for 30 days without a written request from the other parent. Children entering the country without their parents need permits from the Costa Rican embassy in their home country.

Pharmacies

Most towns have a *farmacía* and San
José has many. Most medications are
available over the counter (antibiotics
are a notable exception). Prices are
generally comparable to Western
Europe and Canada, but cheaper
than in the USA. The website
www.medicinavitual.com/farmacias has
a list of pharmacies throughout Costa
Rica. A few stay open 24 hours.

Post

The postal system is often unreliable;
however, the Correo Central (*Central
Post Office, Calle 2, Av 1–3. Tel: (506)
223 9766. www.correos.go.cr. Open:
Mon–Fri 8am–5pm, Sat 7.30am–noon*)
in San José offers international services.
Parcels are subject to customs fees.

Public holidays

Costa Rican *días feriados* (public
holidays) are often connected to
festivals and events. The official public
holidays are:

New Year's Day 1 January
**Thursday and Friday before Easter
Sunday** March/April (these are the
official holidays, but businesses close
during the whole week leading up to
Easter Sunday, which is known as
Semana Santa (Holy Week))
Día de Juan Santamaría 11 April
Día de los Trabajadores (Labour Day)
5 May
Día de la Madre (Mother's Day)
15 August
Independence Day 15 September

Día de la Raza (Columbus Day)
12 October
Christmas Day 25 December
(Christmas Eve and the week between
Christmas and New Year are unofficial
holidays and businesses close).

Reading and media

Factual

Les Beletsky, *Costa Rica: Ecotraveller's
Wildlife Guide* (Academia Press)
Detailed but readable wildlife guide.
Mario A. Boza, *Costa Rica Parques
Nacionales/National Parks* (San José,
Editorial Heliconia)
A glossy coffee-table book with
beautiful photographs.
Paula Palmer, Juanita Sánchez and
Gloria Mayorga, *Taking Care of Sibö's
Gifts* (San José, Editorarama)
A record of the culture and spiritual
beliefs of the Bribrí people.

Fiction

Carlos Luis Fallas, *Mamita Yunai: el
infierno de las bananeras* (San José)
Written in the 1930s, this seminal novel
portrays life on a banana plantation.
Enrique Jaramillo Levi (ed), *When New
Flowers Bloomed: Short Stories by Women
Writers from Costa Rica and Panama*
(USA, Latin American Review Press)
This collection features short stories by
renowned Costa Rican women writers.
Barbara Ras, *Costa Rica: A Traveller's
Literary Companion* (USA,
Whereabouts Press)
A good introduction to Costa Rican
literature and culture.

General

The Tico Times is Costa Rica's weekly English-language newspaper.

Books, magazines and newspapers in English are sold at San José's Juan Santamaría airport, in some hotel gift shops and at large bookshops in San José.

There is an English-language radio station, 107.5FM, which airs BBC news.

Sustainable tourism

Thomas Cook is a strong advocate of ethical and fairly traded tourism and believes that the travel experience should be as good for the places visited as it is for the people who visit them. That's why we firmly support The Travel Foundation, a charity that develops solutions to help improve and protect holiday destinations, their environment, traditions and culture. To find out what you can do to make a positive difference to the places you travel to and the people who live there, please visit *www.thetravelfoundation.org.uk*

Tax

There is no income tax in Costa Rica; instead, revenue is generated through VAT and import duties. When leaving you will have to pay a $26 departure tax.

Telephone, email and internet

The country code for Costa Rica is *506*. Although international mobile telephones sometimes work, reception is unreliable. Public telephones are widely available and generally operate on a phone card (*tarjeta telefónica*)

system. Many hotels have internet access available to guests and most towns.

Time

Costa Rica is six hours behind Greenwich Mean Time (GMT).

Toilets

There are very few public toilets and they tend to be poor quality, but hotels, restaurants and ranger stations have toilets available for public use, sometimes at a small charge. Toilet paper is often lacking and usually should be binned rather than flushed.

Travellers with disabilities

Trails in national parks and wildlife reserves are not generally wheelchair accessible, but there are notable exceptions, including Parque Nacional Volcán Poás and INBioparque. The Foundation for Universal Access to Nature (*Tel: (506) 771 7482. Email: chabote@racsa.co.cr*) gives further information. Serendipity Adventures (*see p171*) tailors activities to individual needs and abilities. Some hotels and lodges have wheelchair access and adapted facilities, but they are in the minority. The companies Vaya con Sella de Ruedas (*Tel: (506) 454 2810. www.gowithwheelchairs.com*) and The Association of Costa Rican Special Taxis (*Tel: (506) 296 6443*) have equipped vans. Contact the Costa Rica Deaf Travel Corporation (*Tel: (506) 289 4812. www.cdtcsa.com*) to enquire about guided sign-language tours.

Language

Costa Rican Spanish does not differ much from the Spanish spoken in Spain, but there are a few noticeable differences. The soft 'c' and the letter 'z' are pronounced as an English letter 's' instead of the 'th' sound heard in Spain. In many situations where the Spanish would use the informal '*tú*' for 'you', Ticos will often stick with the formal address of '*usted*'. English is fairly widely spoken, particularly in the Caribbean region and in popular tourist destinations throughout the country, but if you take the time to learn some Spanish your efforts will undoubtedly prove useful and be welcomed.

Costa Rican	Pronunciation	English
Hola	*oh*-lah	Hello/Hi
Buenos días	*bweh*-nohs *dee*-ahs	Good morning
Buenas tardes	*bweh*-nass *tahr*-dehs	Good afternoon
Buenas noches	*bweh*-nass *noh*-chehs	Good night
Hasta luego	as-ta *lwey*-go	Bye/See you soon
Adiós	a-*dyos*	Goodbye (also colloquially 'Hi')
Sí	see	Yes
No	noh	No
Por favor	pohr fa-*vohr*	Please
Gracias	*grah*-see-ahs	Thank you

Costa Rican	Pronunciation	English
De nada/Con mucho gusto	de *na*-da/con *moo*-cho *goos*-to	You're welcome
Perdón	per-*dohn*	Excuse me

Con permiso	con per-*mee*-so	Excuse me/May I?
Lo siento/Disculpe	lo *syen*-to/dees-*kool*-pe	Sorry
Pura vida	*poo*-ra *vee*-da	*'Pure life'* (approval/greeting)
¿Habla inglés?	*ah*-blah een-*glehs*	Do you speak English?
No hablo español	no *ah*-blo es-pa-*nyol*	I don't speak Spanish
(No) Entiendo	(no) en-*tyen*-do	I (don't) understand
¿Comó está usted?	*koh*-moh ehs-*tah* oos-*tehd*	How are you?
¿Que tal?	ke tal	How are things?
Muy bien gracias	mwee bee-*en gra*-syas	Very well thank you
Mucho gusto	*moo*-cho *goo*-sto	It's a pleasure (to meet you)
Quiero/Quisiera…	kee-*er*-o/kee-*sye*-ra	I want/I would like…
La cuenta por favor	la *kwen*-ta por fa-*vohr*	The bill, please
Soy vegetariano/a	soy ve-heh-ta-ree-*ah*-no/na	I am a vegetarian
Soy alérgico/a a…	soy a-*ler*-khee-ko/a a…	I'm allergic to…
¿Cuánto cuesta?	*kwan*-to *kwes*-ta	How much is it?
¿A que hora abre/cierra?	a ke *o*-ra *a*-bre/*sye*-ra	What time does it open/close
Estoy enfermo/a	es-*toy* en-*fer*-mo/a	I'm ill/sick
¿Dónde está (el baño)?	*don*-de es-*ta* (el *ba*-nyo)	Where is (the toilet)
¡Socorro!	so-*ko*-ro	Help!
¿Cómo llego a…?	*ko*-mo *ye*-go a	How do I get to…?
La izquierda	la ees-*kyer*-da	Left
La derecha	la de-*re*-cha	Right
Estoy perdido/a	es-*toy* per-*dee*-do/a	I'm lost

Emergencies

Crime and scams

While the vast majority of travellers will not experience any crime or scams in Costa Rica, it is wise to be alert. Pickpockets represent the most common risk. Do not wear noticeable jewellery or carry much money or your passport (take a photocopy and leave the original with any valuables in your hotel safe). Do not leave any belongings in parked cars or on beaches. Avoid walking alone after dark. Recently there has been a spate of muggings in San José, concentrated mainly in certain neighbourhoods. Ask advice at your hotel before venturing to any unfamiliar districts. A common scam involves thieves making slow punctures in hire-car wheels and then robbing drivers after offering help. To avoid this and other car crimes, aim to pull over in a well-lit public place if there is a problem or if you are lost.

Embassies

Australia No embassy in Costa Rica, but the Canadian embassy offers consular assistance to Australian citizens.
Canada *Oficentro Ejecutivo La Sabana, Edificio 5, Sabana Sur, San José. Tel: (506) 242 4400.*
New Zealand *Jaime Balmes #8, Level 4, Colonia Los Morales, Polanco, 11510 Mexico City. Tel: (+ 52 55) 283 9460. Fax: (+ 52 55) 283 9480. Email: kiwimexico@prodigy.net.mx*

South Africa *Andres bello 10, 9th Floor, Forum Building, Colonia Polanco, C.P. 11560, Mexico City (postal address: Embajada de Sudafrica, Apartado Postal 105-219, Colonia Polanco, C.P. 11560, Mexico City). Tel: (+ 525 55) 282 9260–65. Fax: (+ 525 55) 282 9259/9186.*
UK *Centro Colón, Paseo Colón, Calles 38/40, San José. Tel: (506) 258 2025.*
USA *Boulevard Rohrmoser, San José. Tel: (506) 220 3939.*

Emergency numbers

911 – All emergencies (ambulance, fire and police)
118 – Fire
117 – Police
128 – Red Cross (Rojo Cruz)
113 – Directory assistance

Health risks and health care

One health risk is the tropical sun, the strength of which should not be underestimated. Drink plenty of water to avoid becoming dehydrated. Contact a doctor if you suspect heatstroke (the symptoms are thirst, nausea, dizziness and fever). There are no compulsory vaccinations, but immunisations against typhoid and hepatitis A are recommended. Malaria is present in a few provinces (Guanacaste, Limón, Heredia and Alajuela), with the biggest risk in the southern part of Limón province. Anti-malarial chloroquine pills are advisable for affected areas.

Some mosquitoes carry dengue fever (a viral infection with symptoms similar to flu), for which there is no vaccine or medication. Fortunately, although there are occasional outbreaks of this, very few travellers are affected. Although it is difficult to avoid mosquito bites altogether, take precautions. In the unlikely event of a snake bite, seek medical attention immediately.

Snakes seldom attack unless provoked, so watch your step, wear solid boots in forest areas and hike with a knowledgeable guide. Bites or scratches by any wild animals should be cleaned and have antiseptic applied straightaway, then seek medical advice, as there is a risk of infection and a negligible but relevant risk of rabies.

Tap water is technically potable in most areas, although it is always best to check locally. Exceptions are the port cities of Puerto Limón and Puntarenas, where it is not safe to drink the tap water.

Useful health advice websites:
www.doh.gov.uk/travellers and
www.fco.gov.uk/travel – health/travel advice for British citizens.
www.cdc.gov/travel and
www.healthfinder.com – geared towards American travellers.
www.travelhealth.co.uk – useful tips and information for British travellers.
www.who.int/en – website of the World Health Organization.
www.tripprep.com – website of Travel Health Online.

www.brookes.ac.uk/worldwise – basic travel information on destinations.

Insurance

Make sure that you are covered by a comprehensive insurance policy. Several of the sports popular in Costa Rica, such as white-water rafting, are often considered 'dangerous' by insurance companies and excluded from basic policies, so you may need additional cover.

Police

The police force is divided into various branches. At the time of writing, a new tourist division had just been inaugurated and was set to grow in numbers. These officers, all of whom have studied English as part of their training, are deployed in popular tourist areas to increase security and assist visitors with directions and information.

Check your insurance policy if you want to go white-water rafting

Directory

Accommodation price guide

For the accommodation and eating out listings in this directory a star rating system indicates the price range. Although the local currency is colones, prices are given here in US dollars, which are also accepted.
Accommodation costs are for an average double room per night.

★	up to US$40
★★	US$40–60
★★★	US$60–100
★★★★	Over US$100

Eating out price guide

For restaurants the price ranges are based on an average-priced main-course meal from the menu, without drinks.

★	US$2–6
★★	US$7–10
★★★	US$11–15
★★★★	Over US$16

SAN JOSÉ
Central
ACCOMMODATION
Gran Hotel de Costa Rica ★★★
This comfortable hotel has been recognised as a national monument and much of the original architecture remains. Ideal for seeing sights. Wheelchair access.
Calle 3, Av Central–2.
Tel: (506) 221 4000. www.grandhotelcostarica.com

EATING OUT
El Patio Del Balmoral ★
Cheerful & central bar-restaurant, attached to the Hotel Balmoral; breakfast, lunch, dinner, drinks and snacks.
Av Central (pedestrianised section). Open: 6am–11pm (later Fri & Sat).
Nuestra Tierra ★
Welcoming, rustic aspect. Classic Costa Rican food.
Corner of Av 2 & Calle 15. Open: 24hrs.

ENTERTAINMENT
Complejo Salsa 54 y Zadidas
Popular Latin dance club for salsa and merengue.
Calle 3, Av 1–3.
Tel: (506) 233 3814.

Barrio Amón and around (northeast)
ACCOMMODATION
Hotel Santo Tomás ★★★
Charming family-oriented hotel in an old colonial mansion. Courtyard garden with swimming pool. Rooms are simple and comfortable. Breakfast and free internet access are included.
Calle 3–5, Av 11.
Tel: (506) 255 0448.
www.hotelsantotomas.com
Clarion Amón Plaza ★★★★
An elegant and comfortable hotel with comprehensive facilities. Wheelchair access.
Calle 3, Av 11.
Tel: (506) 257 0191.
www.hotelamonplaza.com

EATING OUT
Aya Sofya ★★
Enjoy traditional

Turkish food and a belly-dancing party every other weekend.
Av Central, Calle 21.
Tel: (506) 221 7185.
Open: 11.30am–3pm & 6–11pm Mon–Fri, 11.30am–midnight Sat.

El Oasis (Hotel Santo Tomás) ★★
European classics and some Costa Rican dishes are prepared with understated elegance. Seafood and pasta are specialities and highly recommended.
Calle 3, Av 11.
Tel: (506) 257 0191.
Open: 4–11pm Tue–Sat, 3–11pm Sun.

La Cocina de Leña ★★
'The wood oven' is designed in a rustic style, with live *marimba* music on some nights and country décor to match the traditional menu. The food, from steak to black bean soup, is good quality.
Centro Comercial El Pueblo. Tel: (506) 223 3704. Open: 11am–11pm Sun–Thur, 11am–midnight Fri–Sat.

Tin Jo ★★★
Popular gourmet Asian fusion restaurant,

booking recommended.
Calle 11, Av 6–8.
Tel: (506) 221 7605.
Open: 11.30am 3pm & 5.30–10.00pm Mon–Thur, 11.30am–3pm & 5.30–11.00pm Fri–Sat, 11.30am–10pm Sun.

ENTERTAINMENT
Centro Comercial El Pueblo
The El Pueblo complex is a popular spot to drink and dance after dark; several of the bars showcase live music. Acoustic and folk at Los Balcones and Café Boruca (both free entry), tango at Bar Tango Che Molinari (cover charge).

SPORT AND LEISURE
Escapes Ecologicos
Customised tours with knowledgeable guides throughout Costa Rica and to Nicaragua and Panama. Options include ecological, adventure and cultural trips as well as various other packages (including weddings). For Poás tour, *see p46*.
Barrio Amón.
Tel: (506) 257 4566.
www.escapesecologicos.com

La Sábana/Pavas/ Rohrmoser (west)
ACCOMMODATION
Hotel Casa Roland ★★
This hotel is full of character. The unprepossessing building hides a warm, artistically designed interior. Breakfast and free internet access included.
Tel: (506) 231 6571.
www.casa-roland.com

EATING OUT
Soda Tapia ★
This large *soda* (*see p 139*) is reliable for a snack at any time of day.
Corner of Av 2 and Calle 42. Open: 6am–midnight.

El Fogoncito ★★
Filling Mexican-style food (with vegetarian options). Good for families. There is another branch in San Pedro.
Blvd Rohmoser, opposite Plaza Mayor. Tel: (506) 290 0910. Open daily for breakfast, lunch and dinner and until 2am.

Machu Picchu ★★
Popular Peruvian eatery specialising in seafood.
Calle 32, Av 1–3.
Tel: (506) 222 7384.
Open: Mon–Sat 11am–3pm & 6–10pm.

ENTERTAINMENT

Sala Garbo

Art-house cinema, international films.
Av 2, Calle 28.
Tel: (506) 222 1034.

SPORT AND LEISURE

Parque Metropolitano La Sabana has football pitches and ball-game areas. The Costa Rica Tennis Club (*Tel: (506) 232 1266*), on the south side, has a swimming pool, gym and tennis courts, all open to the public for an inexpensive day fee. A second swimming pool is Olympic-sized and has cheap admission, but is open only *noon–2pm.*

San Pedro and around (east)

ACCOMMODATION

Hostel Bekuo ★

Attractive hostel with dorm and private rooms and good shared facilities including kitchen, hot-water bathrooms and free internet access.
Av 8, Calle 39–41.
Tel: (506) 234 1091/ 234 5486.
www.hostelbekuo.com

EATING OUT

Comida Para Sentir ★

Unpretentious student hangout with delicious organic veggie food including fresh juices, soups, salads and local specialities such as heart of palm. Recommended for a weekday lunch (*closed weekends*). Vegan options.
125 N Iglesia Católica San Pedro de Montes de Oca.
Tel: (506) 224 1163.
Open: Mon–Fri 10.30am–6pm.

ENTERTAINMENT

Cines del América

Cinema showing Hollywood and other international films, generally in original language with Spanish subtitles.
Mall San Pedro.
Tel: (506) 222 1034.

El Cuartel de la Boca del Monte

Popular local bar between the city centre and San Pedro, in Barrío California district. There is live Latin, rock or reggae on some nights.
Av 1, Calle 21–23.
Tel: (506) 221 0327.

Jazz Café

Nightly live music at this popular bohemian venue. Some internationally renowned musicians have played here.
Next to Banco Popular, San Pedro.
Tel: (506) 253 8933.
Open: 6pm–2am. Cover charge.

Escazú

ACCOMMODATION

The Alta Hotel ★★★★

Classy boutique hotel decorated in European colonial style. Staggered balconies offer stunning views of the Central Valley beyond a courtyard garden and swimming pool. The restaurant serves gourmet European food with a Caribbean-Cajun twist.
Alto de las Palomas, on the road between Escazú and Santa Ana.
Tel: (506) 282 4160.
www.thealtahotel.com

EATING OUT

Mirador Valle Azul ★★★★

Very upmarket restaurant perched high in the hills. The Italian-French menu is high-quality, but

beware the extortionate wine list. Main attraction is the spectacular view of the city.
San Antonio de Escazú. Tel: (506) 254 6281/214 1708/814 2626.

ENTERTAINMENT
Little Theater Group
English-language drama company. Contact them to find out when and where plays are being performed.
Tel: (506) 289 3910. www. littletheatregroup.com

CENTRAL VALLEY AND HIGHLANDS
Alajuela and north area
ACCOMMODATION
Lagunillas Lodge ★
This value-for-money hotel is the closest to Volcán Poás, just a short distance below the summit. They have *cabinas*, which sleep up to six, and a pond where fishing enthusiasts can catch their own dinner to be cooked by the restaurant staff.
Tel: (506) 448 5506.
Poás Volcano Lodge ★★
This cosy lodge is set on a working dairy

farm and features stone architecture, spacious rooms and fireplaces, communal sitting and games rooms, walking trails through the surrounding forest and mountain bikes for hire. Near Poasito village, about 16km (10 miles) from the volcano.
Tel: (506) 482 2194. www. poasvolcanolodge.com
Peace Lodge ★★★★
This seriously luxurious lodge manages La Paz Waterfall Gardens. One of the 'Small Distinctive Hotels of Costa Rica' it features stone fireplaces, jacuzzis and waterfall showers. The recommended buffet restaurant is open to visitors to the gardens.
Vara Blanca. Tel: (506) 482 2720. www. waterfallgardens.com

EATING OUT
Ambrosia ★
Lively open-air café with a good range of cakes as well as lunches.
Av 5, Calle 2, Alajuela. Open: 9.30am–8pm.
Cugini Bar & Restaurant ★★
Italian-style food in a

casual, comfortable atmosphere. Open until midnight, serving beer and cocktails.
Av Central, Calle 5, Alajuela. Tel: (506) 440 6893.

SPORT AND LEISURE
Ojo de Agua
This family leisure resort with swimming pools, boating lake and games courts is about 6km (4 miles) south of Alajuela. Very busy at weekends.
Tel: (506) 441 2808. Open: 8am–5pm.

Heredia area
ACCOMMODATION
Hotel Heredia ★
Pleasant, leafy, budget hotel with the country charm of Heredia. Solar-heated showers in each private bathroom.
Calle 6, Av 3–5. Tel: (506) 238 0880.

EATING OUT
Vishnu Mango Verde ★
Part of a chain with several branches in San José, this vegetarian café makes a healthy lunch stop.
Calle 7, Av Central–1,

*Heredia. Open: Mon–Sat
9am–6pm.*

La Casa de Doña Lela ★★
This authentic *soda*,
popular with locals, is
ideal for a hearty *casado*
(*see p139*).
*Road to Braulio Carrillo.
Tel: (506) 240 2228.
Open: daily
7.30am–9.30pm.*

Restaurant Fresas ★★
Popular with Heredia's
student population. Does
a range of local dishes,
salads and milkshakes.
*Av 1, Calle 7. Open:
8am–midnight.*

ENTERTAINMENT
Océanos Bar
Lively watersports-
themed bar serving *bocas*
(*see p139*) and featuring
live music at weekends.
*Calle 4, Av 2–4, Heredia.
Tel: (506) 260 7809.
Open: 11am–midnight.*

Cartago area
ACCOMMODATION
**Finca la Flor de
Paraíso ★★**
This organic farm on the
edge of La Flor near
Paraíso sleeps guests in
private rooms (guided
day hikes included), in
addition to hosting

volunteer programmes
and the Alternative
Spanish Institute.
www.la-flor-de-paraiso.org

EATING OUT
La Puerta del Sol ★
Opposite the basilica,
Cartago's main attraction,
is this pleasant *soda* (*see
p139*) with a varied menu.
Open: 8am–midnight.

Turrialba area
ACCOMMODATION
Hotel Turrialtico ★★★
About 8km (5 miles)
outside Turrialba, this
long-established, family-
run lodge set in an old
farmhouse building is an
inviting place to stay.
Beautiful views of the
surrounding countryside.
*Tel: (506) 538 1111.
www.turrialtico.com*

EATING OUT
Café Gourmet ★
This charming Turrialba
café specialises in a range
of coffees and also does
snacks and breakfast.
*Av 4, Calle 2–4.
Tel: (506) 556 9689.*

Restaurant Don Porfi ★★
Locally renowned
restaurant about 4km
(2½ miles) north of

Turrialba (on the way to
San José), serving tasty
European-inspired food.
*Tel: (506) 556 9797.
Open: 10am–10pm.*

SPORT AND LEISURE
**Fundación Ríos
Tropicales**
Arranges white-water
rafting trips of one
to three days on the
Río Pacuare and
provides general
rafting information.
*Tel: (506) 233 6455.
www.riostropicales.com*

**CENTRAL PACIFIC
AND SOUTHERN
NICOYA**
**Puntarenas and
southern Nicoya
Peninsula**
ACCOMMODATION
Hotel La Punta ★
The rooms at this well-
priced little hotel, located
near the ferry terminal, all
have balconies, fans/air-
conditioning and hot-
water bathrooms. There is
a pool, restaurant and bar.
*Av 1, Calle 35, Puntarenas.
Tel: (506) 661 1900/0696.*
**Star Mountain Eco-
Resort ★★★**
Cosy family-run lodge,
built in harmony with the

forest that surrounds it, adjacent to Cabo Blanco Reserve near Mal Pais. Lovely verdant views. *Tel: (506) 640 0101. www. starmountaineco.com*

EATING OUT
La Casona ★
A good bet for generous portions of soup or *casado* (*see p140*) at lunchtime. *Av 1, Calle 9, Puntarenas.*
Casa de los Mariscos ★★
Enjoy an ocean view and fresh seafood here. *Paseo de Turistas, Puntarenas. Tel: (506) 661 1666.*
El Sano Banano Natural Foods Restaurant and Coffee Shop ★★
Organic international dishes (vegetarian, seafood, chicken) and fresh fruit juices. *Montezuma. Tel: (506) 642 0638. www.elbanano.com*
Nectar Bar and Restaurant ★★★★
Gourmet Asian-fusion restaurant with romantic beachside setting. Order sushi at the bar for a more casual experience. *Florblanca Resort, Playa Santa Teresa, Malpaís. Tel: (506) 640 0232.*

ENTERTAINMENT
El Sano Banano
(*see contact details, left*) Features free film screenings each night.
Restaurant Kaite Negro
Popular seafood restaurant with an open-air courtyard. Live music and dancing at weekends. *Av 1, Calle 17, Puntarenas. Tel: (506) 661 2093.*

Central Pacific beaches
ACCOMMODATION
Aparthotel Vista Pacifico ★★
Slightly removed from the bustle of Jacó by a hilltop location, this good-value hotel has great views, well-equipped rooms, lovely garden, pool and barbecue. *Tel: (506) 643 3261. www.vistapacifico.com*
Hotel Villa Caletas ★★★★
One of the 'Small Distinctive Hotels of Costa Rica', with 35 artistically decorated rooms spaced throughout a lush hillside garden in the Punta Leona area between Tárcoles and Jacó. The Amphitheatre

bar (also open to non-guests) faces the ocean. *Tel: (506) 637 0505. www.hotelvillacaletas.com*

EATING OUT
Calinche's Wishbone Eatery ★★
Well-known and high-quality Jacó restaurant with a varied fusion menu. *Tel: (506) 643 3194.*

SPORT AND LEISURE
Kayak Jacó Costa Rica Outriggers
Arranges customised kayaking, sea canoeing and snorkelling trips. *Playa Agujas. Tel: (506) 643 1233. www.kayakjaco.com*

Quepos to Manuel Antonio
ACCOMMODATION
Vista Serena Hostel ★★
Hostelling at its nicest. Price code based on private rooms; dorms also available. Shared kitchen, bathrooms, lounge. Great view. *Located next to the main road between Quepos and Manuel Antonio, on the western side of the road, slightly closer to Quepos*

than to Manuel Antonio.
Tel: (506) 777 5162.
www.vistaserena.com

Mono Azul Hotel ★★★
An oasis of tropical greenery on the main road, with rooms and family-size villas tucked away in landscaped gardens. Children under 12 free. Three swimming pools, library, shop and restaurant. This is the home of Kids Saving the Rainforest, which set up the monkey bridges across the main road and other projects.
Located a short distance outside Quepos, on the road to Manuel Antonio.
Tel: (506) 777 2572. www. hotelmonoazul.com; www. kidssavingtherainforest.org

Hotel Parador ★★★★
Large extravangant hilltop resort with spectacular views of the Pacific. Rooms are comfortable. Facilities include tour desk, spa and tennis courts.
Punta Quepos, Manuel Antonio. Follow signs from the road between Quepos and Manuel Antonio.
Tel: (506) 777 1414.
www.hotelparador.com

EATING OUT

Ronny's Place ★★
Small Tico restaurant perched on a hilltop. Ideal for watching the sun set while sipping a tropical cocktail. The food is traditional and tasty.
Located to the west of the road between Quepos and Manuel Antonio. Follow signs from the main road, between Hostal Vista Serena (on the Manuel Antonio side) and Hotel Mono Azul (on the Quepos side).
Tel: (506) 777 5120.

Barba Roja ★★★
Vibrant bar-restaurant specialising in hearty Mexican-American food. Good vegetarian menu as well as meat and seafood. Extensive cocktail list and daily happy hours (*4.30– 6.30pm*). Live guitar music sometimes played. Open from 6am for breakfast.
Manuel Antonio.
Tel: (506) 777 0331.

SPORT AND LEISURE

Amigo Tico Complete Adventure Tours
Activities including rafting, kayaking, mountain biking and fishing.
Quepos.
Tel: (506) 777 2812.
www.puertoquepos.com

GUANACASTE AND NORTHERN NICOYA
Liberia and north
ACCOMMODATION
Hacienda Los Inocentes ★★
Former cattle ranch near La Cruz, converted and reforested into a biological research station and eco-lodge. Rooms are in an old hacienda building and a few separate *cabinas*. Guided tours in Parque Nacional Guanacaste can be arranged. Meals can be included at additional charge (rating based on accommodation only).
Tel: (506) 679 9190. www. losinocenteslodge.com

Hotel El Punto ★★
Good value B&B. The stylishly decorated rooms include private bathrooms and kitchen facilities.
Liberia – Interamericana highway (Av 25 de Julio & Av 2). Tel: (506) 666 8493.

Hacienda Guachipelín ★★★
Set in the grounds of a working cattle ranch near Rincón de la Vieja, this is a good spot to sample Guanacaste culture. Rooms are basic but spacious and comfortable. Meals can be included at additional charge (rating based on accommodation only).
Tel: (506) 666 8075. www.guachipelin.com

EATING OUT
Los Camales ★
Café run by a local women's collective, serving traditional Guanacaste dishes.
Calle Central, Av 7/5, Liberia.
Paso Real ★★★
The best-known restaurant in Liberia specialises in creatively prepared seafood dishes.
Av Central, Calle Central–2. Tel: (506) 666 3455. Open: 11am–10pm.

SPORT AND LEISURE
El Ocotal Diving Safaris
Based at El Ocotal Hotel. PADI certification courses and week-long diving trips to offshore islands.
Tel: (506) 670 0321. www.ocotaldiving.com

Playa Flamingo to Playa Tamarindo
ACCOMMODATION
Hotel Las Tortugas ★★★
Comfortable hotel near Playa Grande designed with turtle protection in mind (light is kept away from the beach). Facilities include a pool and a jacuzzi. Aqua-sports equipment rented. Eleven regular suites and two self-catering apartments.
Tel: (506) 653 0423. www.cool.co.cr/usr/turtles
Capitán Suizo ★★★★
One of the 'Small Distinctive Hotels of Costa Rica' and one of the longest-established Tamarindo hotels, with a perfect beachside location. Gorgeous rooms (standard doubles in main hotel building, deluxe cabins in garden). Wildlife is often seen in the grounds. There is a classy restaurant and candlelit dinners can be arranged on the beach. Live *marimba* music some nights. Facilities include swimming pool, gift shop and tour desk.

Tel: (506) 653 0353/ 653 0075. www. hotelcapitansuizo.com
Bahía del Sol ★★★★
Boutique hotel in a quiet bay near Playa Flamingo. Rooms include family-size fully equipped apartments (children under 12 free). The design is tropical luxury, with gardens, pool, open-air restaurant and swim-up bar.
Potrero Bay, Flamingo. Tel: (506) 654 4671. www.potrerobay.com; www.bahiadelsolhotel.com

EATING OUT
Olga's Coffee Shop ★
Get organic coffee and homemade snacks at this cute café in Tamarindo.
Near Playa Pelada.
Restaurant/Bar Happy Snapper ★★
This beachside restaurant has ocean views, serves seafood and features live music and dancing.
Playa Brasilito. Tel: (506) 654 4413.
Stella's ★★
Italian-style restaurant specialising in pasta, wood-oven pizzas, fresh fish and seafood.
Tamarindo. Tel: (506) 653 0127.

Pachanga ★★★

A romantic restaurant renowned for high-quality gourmet food.
Near Pasatiempo Hotel, Tamarindo.
Tel: (506) 653 0021.
Open: Mon–Sat 6–10pm.

SPORT AND LEISURE

Blue Dolphin Catamarans

The friendly crew of the Blue Dolphin run catamaran sailing and snorkelling trips; drinks and snacks included. The sublime sunset sail is particularly highly recommended.
Playa Tamarindo.
Tel: (506) 653 0867/ 842 3204.
www.sailbluedolphin.com

Witch's Rock Surf Camp

Complete American-style surf culture, including *nachos* and cold beers at the café and excursions.
Tamarindo.
Tel: (506) 653 0239. www. witchsrocksurfcamp.com

Central peninsula and beaches

ACCOMMODATION

Tico Adventure Lodge ★★

This delightful, great-value lodge was built around the trees on the site. Nine double rooms, a treetop apartment for four and a poolside house for five (with kitchen).
Playa Sámara.
Tel: (506) 656 0628. www. ticoadventurelodge.com

Lagarta Lodge Biological Reserve ★★★

Luxury hilltop lodge with stunning views of the ocean and Reserva Biológica Nosara. Good wildlife-spotting opportunities. Restaurant serves local and international options.
Nosara. Tel: (506) 682 0035. www.lagarta.com

EATING OUT

Soda Ananas ★

Open for breakfast, lunch and afternoon coffee, this café features smoothies and ice cream.
Sámara (at the entrance to town).
Tel: (506) 656 0491.

La Luna ★★★

Sophisticated terrace restaurant-bar features a varied international fusion menu with Thai and Mediterranean food.
Playa Pelada (Nosara).
Tel: (506) 682 0122.
Open: 11am–11pm.

ENTERTAINMENT

La Vela Latina

Trendy beach bar serving *bocas* (bar snacks) to soak up the blended cocktails and sangria.
Playa Sámara.

SPORT AND LEISURE

Ciclo Sámara

Bicycle hire shop, which rents bikes by the hour or day for a reasonable rate.
Playa Sámara.
Tel: (506) 656 0438.

Nosara Surf 'n' Sport

Arranges surfing lessons and tours.
Playa Guiones.
Tel: (506) 682 0186.
www.nosarasurfshop.com.
Open: 7am–6pm.

Nosara Yoga Institute

Hillside retreat running yoga classes and workshops.
Near Guiones.
Tel: (506) 682 0071.
www.nosarayoga.com

NORTHERN ZONE

Monteverde and Santa Elena

ACCOMMODATION

Finca Terra Viva ★

A working farm being reforested. Four family-size rustic rooms each have a hot shower. Guests can get involved by milking cows and making cheese.

Between Santa Elena village and reserve.
Tel: (506) 645 5454.
www.terravivacr.com

Sunset Hotel ★★
Cosy hotel rooms have porches and hot showers. Private nature trails and scenic views.
3km (2 miles) northeast of Santa Elena.
Tel: (506) 645 5228.

El Sapo Dorado ★★★★
Graceful hotel consisting of wooden cabins that resemble Alpine chalets. Panoramic views of Golfo de Nicoya. Owns Sendero Tranquilo cloud forest reserve (*see p85*). An excellent gourmet restaurant includes creative vegetarian and vegan options as well as plenty to keep meat-eaters happy.
Tel: (506) 645 5010.
www.sapodorado.com

EATING OUT
Flor de Vida ★★
Unique restaurant, part of a small courtyard complex, which also includes an art gallery

(works by Monteverde artists) and a free theatre. The restaurant has a largely vegetarian menu with a variety of innovative Costa Rican and international dishes on offer.
Tel: (506) 645 6328.
www.flordevida.net.
Open 8am–9/10pm.

Morpho's Restaurant ★★
Traditional Costa Rican staples are given a sophisticated twist here.
Santa Elena.
Tel: (506) 645 5607.
Open: 7.30am–9.30pm.

Tramonti Pizzeria e Ristorante ★★
Classic Italian restaurant; chic but warm.
Tel: (506) 645 6120.

ENTERTAINMENT
Moon Shiva Restaurant
This restaurant (Mediterranean/Middle Eastern-style) is also a popular entertainment venue. Frequent live music nights with a varied programme from rock to salsa.
Cerro Plano.
Tel (506) 645 6270.
Open: 10am–10pm.

SPORT AND LEISURE
Desafio Adventure Company
Well established company with activities in Monteverde and La Fortuna, plus horseback transfer. Desafio is recommended for this trip as their horses are well treated. They offer several scenic horse treks.
Frente Super La Esperanza, Monteverde.
Tel: (506) 645 5874. www. monteverdetours.com

Arenal area
ACCOMMODATION
Cerro Chato Lodge ★
Small eco-lodge involved in a community environmental education project. Rooms have hot-water bathrooms and breakfast is included. Camping facilities available. Horse rides, nature tours and lava tours offered.
Near La Fortuna.
Tel: (506) 479 9494.
www.cerrochato.com

Albergue La Catarata ★★
Run by a co-operative for sustainable tourism. Nine *cabinas* with private hot-water bathrooms.

Guided walks can be arranged. There is a medicinal plant garden and small restaurant.
La Fortuna.
Tel: (506) 479 9522.
www.cataratalodge.com
Lomas del Volcán ★★★
Peaceful hotel with great volcano view. Wooden cabins have private hot-water bathrooms.
West of La Fortuna.
Tel: (506) 479 9000.
www.lomasdelvolcan.com

EATING OUT
Don Rufino ★★
One of the more upmarket restaurants in town, specialising in good-value lunches and gourmet dinners.
Calle Central, La Fortuna.
Tel: (506) 479 9997.
www.donrufino.com.
Open: 11am–10pm.
Restaurant Las Nenes ★★
This popular restaurant specialises in seafood.
Calle 5, La Fortuna.
Tel: (506) 479 9145.
Open: 10am–11pm.

SPORT AND LEISURE
Desafío Adventure Company
Around La Fortuna, exhilarating activities include white-water rafting and kayaking, mountain biking and canyoneering (abseiling) down La Fortuna waterfall.
Behind the church, La Fortuna.
Tel: (506) 479 9464.
www.desafiocostarica.com
Tico Wind
Windsurfing rentals on Lake Arenal from December to mid-April. Lessons for beginners and improvers.
Neear Tilarán.
Tel: (506) 695 5387.
www.ticowind.com
Hotel Tilawa
Hotel with windsurfing and kitesurfing school and rentals.
Near Tilarán.
Tel: (506) 695 5050.
www.hotel-tilawa.com

Northern lowlands
ACCOMMODATION
Tilajari Resort Hotel ★★★
Welcoming hotel in a peaceful location beside Río San Carlos. Sports facilities include pools and tennis courts and the lovely gardens are noteworthy. Offers safari floats on the river and tours including Caño Negro, Volcán Arenal and nearby caves.
Muelle, San Carlos.
Tel: (506) 469 9091.
www.tilajari.com

SPORT AND LEISURE
Sarapiquí Aguas Bravas
Rafting and kayaking on the Río Sarapiquí, plus biking and other activities. Many of their rafting excursions are family-oriented. Pick-up from your hotel.
Tel: (506) 292 2072.
www.aguas-bravas.co.cr
Serendipity Adventures
The only ballooning company in Costa Rica (*see p125*) also designs individual itineraries featuring adventure activities throughout the country. Groups are never combined and each party is designated a guide. Horse riding is offered in conjunction with Centaura Stables, located near Muelle, and is highly recommended for an authentic and enjoyable experience with well-looked-after horses.
Tel: (506) 558 1000.
Centaura Stables
Tel: (506) 474 8557. www. serendipityadventures.com

CARIBBEAN COAST
Tortuguero
ACCOMMODATION
Cabinas Aracari ★
Good-value, comfortable *cabinas*. Private cold-water bathrooms and fans. Lovely garden.
Tel: (506) 709 8006.

Mawamba Lodge ★★★★
On the sliver of land between Tortuguero Lagoon and the sea, this is a luxurious tropical retreat, complete with exotic gardens and private dock. Rustic wood-panelled rooms have hot-water bathrooms. Room rates include all meals, transfers from San José and tours around Tortuguero. There is also a frog sanctuary with resident red-eyed tree frogs.
Tel: (506) 293 8181. www. grupomawamba.com

EATING OUT
Miss Miriam's ★
Bright and breezy restaurant next to the village football pitch. Good traditional Caribbean food. Rooms are available and canoe tours can be arranged.
Tel: (506) 709 8002.

Miss Junie's ★★
Recommended for delectable Caribbean cuisine. Fish and chicken in coconut sauce are specialities. Stop by or ring early in the day to make a reservation. Rooms also available and include breakfast.
Tel: (506) 709 8029. Open: 6–9pm.

SPORT AND LEISURE
The Tortuguero Info Centre
This centre can put you in touch with a local guide for a canal boat trip, turtle tour or hike.
Tel: (506) 709 8055. tortuguero_info@racsa. co.cr

Puerto Limón and central coast
ACCOMMODATION
Cabinas Cocori ★★
Bright hotel with comfortable rooms, between Limón and Moín. Breakfast included, swimming pool, leafy garden and bar-restaurant on the beach.
Playa Bonita. Tel: (506) 795 1670.

EATING OUT
Restaurant Brisas del Caribe ★
Pleasant restaurant with patio and balcony overlooking Parque Vargas. Food is traditional Caribbean-style.
Limón. Tel: (506) 758 0138. Open: Mon–Fri 7am–11pm, Sat & Sun 10am–11pm.

ENTERTAINMENT
Quibamba
Beach bar and restaurant. Good for ocean views, people-watching and fresh seafood. Live music some nights.
Playa Bonita. Tel: (506) 795 4805.

Southern Caribbean
ACCOMMODATION
Cabinas Riverside ★
Cheerful budget option near Kelly Creek entrance to Cahuita Park. Garden with hammocks, rooms have hot-water showers and mosquito nets.
Tel: (506) 553 0153.

Almonds and Corals ★★★★
Lodge/campsite with a seriously luxurious twist in a forest clearing near lovely beach. Deluxe

tents raised on wooden platforms. Facilities include jacuzzi, restaurant, bar and hot-water bathrooms.
Gandoca-Manzanillo. Tel: (506) 271 3000. www. almondsandcorals.com

EATING OUT

Cha Cha Cha! ★★
Enchanting Cahuita restaurant with varied menu including Mexican and Caribbean dishes. Jazz and world music adds to the atmosphere.
Cahuita. Tel: (506) 394 4153. Open: Tue–Sun noon–10pm.

SPORT AND LEISURE

Aquamor Adventures
Environmentally and socially conscientious diving specialist offering tours and courses.
Gandoca-Manzanillo. Tel: (506) 391 3417. www.greencoast.com/ aquamor

SOUTHERN ZONE

Southern mountains

ACCOMMODATION

Talari Mountain Lodge ★★
Charming mountain lodge. Treks to Chirripó

can be organised. Breakfast included.
Rivas, 7km/4 miles south of San Isidro de El General. Tel: (506) 771 0341. www.talari.co.cr

Trogon Lodge ★★★
Alpine-style lodge near Parque Nacional Los Quetzales. Polished wooden cabins overlook a pond, surrounded by cloud forest. Activities include mountain-biking.
San Gerardo de Dota. Tel: (506) 293 8181. www.grupomawamba.com

EATING OUT

Taquería México Lindo ★
Traditional Mexican food (vegetarian options).
Av 2, Calle Central–1, San Isidro de El General. Tel: (506) 771 8222. Open: 10am–8.30pm.

Kafe de la Casa ★★
Artsy café serving breakfast, lunch, snacks and coffees.
Av 3, Calle 2–4, San Isidro de El General. Tel: (506) 770 4816. Open: 7am–8pm.

SPORT AND LEISURE

Costa Rica Trekking Adventures
Multi-day treks in

various parks including Chirripó and Corcovado.
Tel: (506) 771 4582. www.chirripo.com

Dominical and Marino Balleno area

ACCOMMODATION

Cascada Verde ★
Organic farm and retreat near Uvita village. Shared bathrooms. Restaurant serves vegetarian food.
Playa Uvita.

Hacienda Barú Lodge ★★
Eco-lodge with six two-bedroom self-catering cabins in a pristine wildlife refuge north of Dominical. Beaches, mangroves and rainforest are on the doorstep. Restaurant serves typical Costa Rican food. Good for families (children under 11 free).
Tel: (506) 787 0003/0004. www.haciendabaru.com

EATING OUT

Jungle Bistro ★★
Tasty tropical dishes.
Dominical. Tel: (506) 787 0091. Open: 5–11pm.

ENTERTAINMENT

Maracutú
Cheerful beach bar and restaurant featuring

vegetarian and vegan dishes. Different music every night, from reggae to world music. Live music on Sundays. *Dominical. Tel: (506) 811 3611. Open: Sun–Wed 11am–11pm.*

SPORT AND LEISURE
Mystic Dive Centre
Scuba trips in Parque Nacional Marino Ballena. *Playa Ventanas. Tel: (506) 788 8636. www.mysticdivecenter.com*

Península de Osa and Golfo Dulce
ACCOMMODATION
Corcovado Jungle Eco Lodge ★
Inland from Bahía Drake, this bargain lodge has private cabins, lodge rooms, a treehouse and camping facilities, plus a botanical garden and fruit trees. Three organic meals a day for a supplement. *Tel: (506) 770 8209. www. corcovadojungleecolodge. com*
Playa Preciosa Lodge ★★★
Beach lodge with four spacious split-level bungalows and eight platform tents. Breakfast

included and other meals are available. *Playa Platanares, near Puerto Jiménez. Tel: (506) 818 2959. www. playa-preciosa-lodge.com*
Tamandu Lodge ★★★
Run by a Guaymí family on a reserve bordering Corcovado. Guests stay in traditional-style wooden cabins on the farm and learn how to gather and prepare food as the Guaymí do (home-cooked meals included). Two-hour horse ride from La Palma. *Tel: (506) 821 4525. www.tamandu-lodge.com*
Playa Nicuesa Rainforest Lodge ★★★★
This lodge combines luxury with sustainability in the rainforest of Piedras Blancas. Beautifully crafted wooden rooms and cabins with balcony and porch, open-air solar-heated bathroom, fan and mosquito net. Children aged six and over welcomed. The excellent chef caters specially for vegetarians and dietary requirements. Communal dining room and bar area. Guests are collected

from Golfito or Puerto Jiménez by boat. Guided activities and tours. *Tel: (506) 222 0704. www.nicuesalodge.com. Closed: Nov.*

EATING OUT
Pollosa ★★
Specialities are roast chicken, salads, sandwiches and pasta. Takeaway is available. *Puerto Jiménez. Tel: (506) 735 5667. Open: Sun–Fri noon–9pm.*
Il Giardino ★★★
Homemade pasta, fresh seafood and pizzas at breezy garden restaurant. *Puerto Jiménez. Tel: (506) 735 5129. Open: 10am–2pm & 5–10pm.*

SPORT AND LEISURE
Corcovado Expeditions
Tours to Corcovado and Isla del Caño, speciality bird, frog and biking tours, plus bike rentals. *Tel: (506) 818 9962. www. corcovadoexpeditions.net*
Osa Aventura
Specialist in Corcovado treks and tours. *Puerto Jiménez. Tel: (506) 735 5670. www.osaaventura.com*

Index

Acknowledgements

Thomas Cook wishes to thank the photographer, DANNY LEVY SHEEHAN, for the loan of the photographs reproduced in this book, to whom copyright in the photographs belongs (except the following):

DESAFIO ADVENTURE COMPANY 26, 86, 92, 93
PICTURES COLOUR LIBRARY 142, 144
SERENDIPITY ADVENTURES COSTA RICA 24, 125
TRAVEL EXCELLENCE 14, 17, 18, 75, 97, 100, 102, 121, 122, 123, 141, 142, 147
WORLD PICTURES 1, 143

Copy-editing: LYNN BRESLER for CAMBRIDGE PUBLISHING MANAGEMENT LTD

Index: KAROLIN THOMAS for CAMBRIDGE PUBLISHING MANAGEMENT LTD

Maps: PCGRAPHICS (UK) LTD, Old Woking, UK

Proofreading: JAN McCANN for CAMBRIDGE PUBLISHING MANAGEMENT LTD

SEND YOUR THOUGHTS TO
BOOKS@THOMASCOOK.COM

We're committed to providing the very best up-to-date information in our travel guides and constantly strive to make them as useful as they can be. You can help us to improve future editions by letting us have your feedback. If you've made a wonderful discovery on your travels that we don't already feature, if you'd like to inform us about recent changes to anything that we do include, or if you simply want to let us know your thoughts about this guidebook and how we can make it even better – we'd love to hear from you.

Send us ideas, discoveries and recommendations today and then look out for your valuable input in the next edition of this title.

Emails to the above address, or letters to Travellers Project Editor, Thomas Cook Publishing, PO Box 227, Coningsby Road, Peterborough PE3 8SB, UK.

Please don't forget to let us know which title your feedback refers to!